CRIME OR CUSTOM?
Violence Against Women in Pakistan

Human Rights Watch
New York · Washington · London · Brussels

Copyright © August 1999 by Human Rights Watch.
All rights reserved.
Printed in the United States of America.

ISBN: 1-56432-241-6
Library of Congress Card Number: 99-066772

Cover photo by M. Kaursheed (Associated Press). Victims of domestic abuse Nusrat Prveet, 30, right, and Tasneen Bibi, 25, pose in a hospital in Islamabad, Pakistan, September 1997. Parveen had her nose cut off by her husband and Bibi had acid thrown in her face by her in-laws.

Cover design by Rafael Jiménez

Addresses for Human Rights Watch
350 Fifth Avenue, 34th Floor, New York, NY 10118-3299
Tel: (212) 290-4700, Fax: (212) 736-1300, E-mail: hrwnyc@hrw.org

1630 Connecticut Avenue, N.W., Suite 500, Washington, DC 20009
Tel: (202) 612-4321, Fax: (202) 612-4333, E-mail: hrwdc@hrw.org

33 Islington High Street, N1 9LH London, UK
Tel: (171) 713-1995, Fax: (171) 713-1800, E-mail: hrwatchuk@gn.apc.org

15 Rue Van Campenhout, 1000 Brussels, Belgium
Tel: (2) 732-2009, Fax: (2) 732-0471, E-mail:hrwatcheu@skynet.be

Web Site Address: http://www.hrw.org

Listserv address: To subscribe to the list, send an e-mail message to majordomo@igc.apc.org with "subscribe hrw-news" in the body of the message (leave the subject line blank).

Human Rights Watch is dedicated to
protecting the human rights of people around the world.

We stand with victims and activists to prevent
discrimination, to uphold political freedom, to protect people from inhuma
conduct in wartime, and to bring offenders to justice.

We investigate and expose
human rights violations and hold abusers accountable.

We challenge governments and those who hold power to end abusive practi
and respect international human rights law.

We enlist the public and the international
community to support the cause of human rights for all.

HUMAN RIGHTS WATCH

Human Rights Watch conducts regular, systematic investigations of human rights abuses in some seventy countries around the world. Our reputation for timely, reliable disclosures has made us an essential source of information for those concerned with human rights. We address the human rights practices of governments of all political stripes, of all geopolitical alignments, and of all ethnic and religious persuasions. Human Rights Watch defends freedom of thought and expression, due process and equal protection of the law, and a vigorous civil society; we document and denounce murders, disappearances, torture, arbitrary imprisonment, discrimination, and other abuses of internationally recognized human rights. Our goal is to hold governments accountable if they transgress the rights of their people.

Human Rights Watch began in 1978 with the founding of its Europe and Central Asia division (then known as Helsinki Watch). Today, it also includes divisions covering Africa, the Americas, Asia, and the Middle East. In addition, it includes three thematic divisions on arms, children's rights, and women's rights. It maintains offices in New York, Washington, Los Angeles, London, Brussels, Moscow, Dushanbe, Rio de Janeiro, and Hong Kong. Human Rights Watch is an independent, nongovernmental organization, supported by contributions from private individuals and foundations worldwide. It accepts no government funds, directly or indirectly.

The staff includes Kenneth Roth, executive director; Michele Alexander, development director; Reed Brody, advocacy director; Carroll Bogert, communications director;Cynthia Brown,program director; Barbara Guglielmo, finance director; Jeri Laber special advisor; Lotte Leicht, Brussels office director; Patrick Minges, publications director; Susan Osnos, associate director; Maria Pignataro Nielsen, human resources director; Jemera Rone, counsel; Wilder Tayler, general counsel; and Joanna Weschler, United Nations representative. Jonathan Fanton is the chair of the board. Robert L. Bernstein is the founding chair.

The regional directors of Human Rights Watch are Peter Takirambudde, Africa; José Miguel Vivanco, Americas; Sidney Jones, Asia; Holly Cartner, Europe and Central Asia; and Hanny Megally, Middle East and North Africa. The thematic division directors are Joost R. Hiltermann, arms; Lois Whitman, children's; and Regan Ralph, women's.

The members of the board of directors are Jonathan Fanton, chair; Lisa Anderson, Robert L. Bernstein, David M. Brown, William Carmichael, Dorothy Cullman, Gina Despres, Irene Diamond, Adrian W. DeWind, Fiona Druckenmiller, Edith Everett, Michael E. Gellert, Vartan Gregorian, Alice H. Henkin, James F. Hoge, Stephen L. Kass, Marina Pinto Kaufman, Bruce Klatsky, Joanne Leedom-Ackerman, Josh Mailman, Yolanda T. Moses, Samuel K. Murumba, Andrew Nathan, Jane Olson, Peter Osnos, Kathleen Peratis, Bruce Rabb, Sigrid Rausing, Orville Schell, Sid Sheinberg, Gary G. Sick, Malcolm Smith, Domna Stanton, and Maya Wiley. Robert L. Bernstein is the founding chair of Human Rights Watch.

ACKNOWLEDGMENTS

This report was researched and written by Samya Burney and edited by Regan E. Ralph and Cynthia Brown. The chapter on the international community's response was written by Kerry McArthur. Invaluable research and editorial input were contributed by Kerry McArthur, Kinsey Dinan, and Patricia Gossman. The report follows a 1992 report, *Double Jeopardy: Police Abuse of Women in Pakistan*, which documented sexual abuse of women by state agents.

The women's rights division of Human Rights Watch gratefully acknowledges the assistance of the many individuals, government officials, and institutions in Pakistan who were instrumental in our efforts to investigate the barriers to justice faced by women victims of violence in Pakistan. Our work would not have been possible without the courageous women who were willing to speak to us of their experiences in seeking redress for abuse and assault through the criminal justice system in Pakistan. We would like to extend our particular thanks to human rights attorney Hina Jilani, who has been a key source of support and encouragement since the inception of this project. We would also like to thank the staff of War Against Rape, Shirkat Gah, the Human Rights Commission of Pakistan, Lawyers for Human Rights and Legal Aid, and AGHS Legal Aid Cell for their critical assistance. In addition, we are grateful to the staff of the Police Surgeon's Office, Karachi, Justice Dr. Ghous Muhammad of the Sindh High Court, Julie Chadbourne, Nadeem Fazil Ayaz, Sohail A. Warraich, Zia Awan, Danish Zuberi, Muhammad Ali, Mahboob Khan, and Nausheen Ahmed for their invaluable help.

The women's rights division of Human Rights Watch gratefully acknowledges the support of the Sandler Family Supporting Fund, the John D. and Catherine T. MacArthur Foundation, the Ford Foundation, the Moriah Fund, and the Shaler Adams Foundation.

TABLE OF CONTENTS

I. SUMMARY 1

II. RECOMMENDATIONS 6

III. BACKGROUND 18

IV. PAKISTAN'S OBLIGATIONS UNDER INTERNATIONAL LAW ... 26

V. THE SCOPE OF THE PROBLEM OF VIOLENCE
    AGAINST WOMEN 29

VI. THE STATE RESPONSE TO VIOLENCE AGAINST WOMEN 33
    Domestic Law 33
        Rape 33
        Domestic Violence 40
    Gender Bias in the Criminal Justice System 45
    Role of the Police 52
        Delayed and Mishandled Processing of Complaints 52
        Harassment and Abuse of Victims 57
        Inadequate and Improper Investigations 59
    Medicolegal Examinations 63
        Importance of Forensic Evidence in Cases of Sexual
            Assault and Domestic Violence 63
        Late Referrals and Other Police Delays 65
        Inaccessibility of Doctors 68
        Lack of Training of Medicolegal Personnel 72
        Inadequate Equipment and Facilities 77
        Inadequate and Abusive Examinations. Sexual
            Assault Cases 80
            Purpose of Medicolegal Examination 80
            Inappropriate Focus on Virginity Status 82
            Haphazard Procedures 86
            Mistreatment of Victims 87
        Inadequate and Abusive Exams: Adultery
            or Fornication Cases 89
    Role of the Office of the Chemical Examiner 90
    Use of Medical Evidence at Trial 92

VII. THE RESPONSE OF THE INTERNATIONAL COMMUNITY 95
    The United States 95

    Other Bilateral Assistance 96
    The European Union 96
    International Financial Institutions 96
    The United Nations 98

VIII. CONCLUSION 100

I. SUMMARY

On April 6, 1999, twenty-seven-year-old Samia Sarwar was gunned down in her attorneys' office in Lahore by a hit man retained by her family. Her mother, father, and paternal uncle were all accomplices to her murder. Ms. Sarwar was killed because she was seeking a divorce from her estranged husband—an action her family deemed "dishonorable" and, hence, warranting death. That Ms. Sarwar suffered such drastic consequences for asserting a modicum of independence is not surprising in Pakistan, where the practice of so-called honor killing claims the lives of hundreds of women every year. Ms. Sarwar's transgression, in the eyes of her family, was seeking a divorce; other women are attacked, by or at the instigation of family members, for choosing their spouses. In addition, countless women suffer from battery, rape, burning, acid attacks, and mutilation. Estimates of the percentage of women who experience spousal abuse alone range from 70 to upwards of 90 percent. If there is anything more disturbing than the prevalence of these crimes, it is the impunity with which they are committed. Samia Sarwar's case is an example not only of the violence experienced by Pakistani women but also of the lack of governmental will to do anything about it. As this report went to print, months after her murder, Ms. Sarwar's killers had still not been brought to trial despite exceptionally strong and credible evidence against them. Similarly, of 215 cases of women being suspiciously burned to death in their Lahore homes in 1997, in only six cases were suspects even taken into custody.

Women in Pakistan face staggeringly high rates of rape, sexual assault, and domestic violence while their attackers largely go unpunished owing to rampant incompetence, corruption, and biases against women throughout the criminal justice system. Women who report rape or sexual assault encounter a series of obstacles. These include not only the police, who resist filing their claims and misrecord their statements, but also medicolegal doctors, who focus on their virginity status and lack the training and supplies to conduct adequate examinations. As for the trial in rape cases, typically, in the words of a Lahore district attorney, "The past sexual history of the victim is thrown around and touted in court to the maximum." Furthermore, women who file rape charges open themselves up to the possibility of being prosecuted for illicit sex if they fail to "prove" rape under the 1979 Hudood Ordinances, which criminalize adultery and fornication. As a result, when women victims of violence resort to the judicial system for redress, they are more likely to find further abuse and victimization.

Women victims of domestic violence encounter even higher levels of unresponsiveness and hostility, as actors at all levels of the criminal justice system typically view domestic violence as a private matter that does not belong in the courts. Police respond to domestic violence charges by trying to reconcile the concerned parties rather than filing a report and arresting the perpetrator, and the few women who are referred to medicolegal doctors for examination are evaluated by skeptical physicians who lack any training in the collection of forensic evidence. When asked about the domestic violence victims who have been examined at his office, the head medicolegal doctor for Karachi explained that "25 percent of such women come with self-inflicted wounds."

Human Rights Watch has investigated the Pakistan government's response to the pervasive problem of violence against women in the country's two largest cities, Karachi and Lahore. Despite the severity of the problem, the government's response has been indifferent at best. At worst it has served to exacerbate the suffering of women victims of violence and to obstruct the course of justice. Our findings highlight that a grossly inadequate and discriminatory legal framework is only one of a whole series of hurdles for victims seeking redress. Victims also have to contend with biased officials and outright harassment at every step of the law enforcement process, from the initial registering of a complaint to the trial. Only the most persistent and resourceful complainants succeed in maneuvering such hostile terrain, and even those who do seldom see their attackers punished.

In the course of our investigation, we interviewed human rights lawyers and activists, police officials, medicolegal doctors, the personnel of government forensic laboratories, prosecutors, judges, and women victims of violence who had attempted to navigate the criminal justice system in order to obtain redress. Our findings are based on these interviews and on-site visits to government hospitals, medicolegal centers, and analytical laboratories.

Human Rights Watch examined the state response to sexual violence outside the home as well as to sexual and other violence by intimate partners. However, this report deals primarily with the former because we were unable to identify even one domestic violence victim whose criminal complaint had been registered by the police. We found that, with the exception of the rare high-profile incident, domestic violence cases were virtually never investigated or prosecuted. In fact, Pakistani law fails to criminalize a common and serious form of domestic violence: marital rape. Even complaints regarding acts of domestic violence that fall within the ambit of the criminal law, such as assault or attempted murder, are routinely ignored or downplayed by the police as a result of biased attitudes and ignorance and lack of training with respect to the scope of the law. Such resistance on the part of the police to recognize domestic violence as a crime allows the battering of women to continue with impunity and contributes to a climate that deters women from reaching out for safety and justice.

Although the most determined and resilient complainants in cases of non-familial sexual violence fare marginally better in terms of getting access to the judicial system, they face an extremely adverse legal regime. A stark example of the serious flaws in the applicable legislation is the fact that the very filing of rape charges can make the victim vulnerable to prosecution for extramarital sex. In some instances victims of rape and sexual abuse have actually been detained for months or even years, prior to trial, on charges of illicit sexual intercourse. Since statutory rape is not a crime in Pakistan, even barely pubescent girls alleging rape risk being charged with fornication or consensual sex outside of marriage. The possibility of prosecution, especially in a context where women victims of sexual violence are routinely disrespected and disbelieved by state officials, serves strongly to inhibit victims from pressing charges.

Sexual violence victims' first contact with the law enforcement system generally occurs at the police station. Here, right from the start, they typically encounter rejection of their complaints and harassment. The station chief of a busy Lahore police station told Human Rights Watch that rape did not exist in Pakistani society. He stated his belief that in practically all cases of alleged rape, women had consented to the act of intercourse and then lied to incriminate their male partners. These sentiments were echoed by several other police officers interviewed by Human Rights Watch. Given the prevalence of such biased attitudes among officials, it is not surprising that women complainants are consistently turned away from police stations and, at times, are even intimidated or warned against attempting to file charges. The police also intervene, often at the behest of the accused, to try to force the concerned parties to reach a settlement without officially registering a complaint. When a complaint is registered, usually through herculean efforts on behalf of the victim, any follow-up by the police is generally minimal and rudimentary, a mockery of professional investigative methodology. Furthermore, even such limited action by the police usually requires persistent inquiries and pressure from the complainant.

Serious failings also exist in the government's collection and analysis of medicolegal evidence, which is a practical prerequisite for securing convictions in cases of sexual assault. In many cases, police unnecessarily delay informing women of the necessity of a medicolegal examination and giving them the official referrals required for this purpose. This consistent lapse on the part of the police is especially egregious in view of the transient nature of forensic medical evidence and its critical importance in cases of sexual assault. Nor do the police ensure, where legitimate and possible, that the accused undergoes a prompt medicolegal evaluation. A timely examination of the accused can yield significant evidence of signs of struggle in cases where the victim resisted the attack, evidence that can be crucial for exonerating the victim from charges of consensual illicit sex.

When medicolegal examinations are performed, they are frequently conducted in a haphazard manner and fail to secure meaningful evidence. Doctors focus on determining whether and when the hymen was broken rather than on collecting evidence to demonstrate the extent and severity of women's injuries and to identify offenders. In some cases, unmarried women who, in the examining doctors' opinion, were not virgins prior to being attacked tend to be harassed and their rape allegations disbelieved by the doctors. The examination findings also render them vulnerable to attacks on their character by defense counsel and, potentially, to prosecution for prior illicit sex. The focus on the hymen also militates against effective examinations of sexually active married women because their injuries are not usually related to hymenal tearing. In addition to shoddy examinations, chemical analysis of forensic samples collected from the examinees is commonly mishandled and produces unreliable results.

The court system presents its own set of hurdles for women seeking redress. Magistrates and judges often have discriminatory and sexist assumptions about women that prejudice the few cases that do reach the courts. State prosecutors have little or no training in handling cases of sexual and other violence against women and are largely ignorant as to the significance and interpretation of forensic medical evidence in such cases. Judges allow defense counsel free rein to introduce inflammatory evidence and to attack the victim's character and prior sexual history even when this is patently irrelevant. Furthermore, in many instances, cases drag on for years. For a woman seeking redress, her experience with the judicial system is often more likely to compound the trauma of the original assault than to provide the satisfaction of seeing justice done.

Pakistan is obliged by its ratification of international treaties to ensure respect for women's human rights and fundamental freedoms. The Convention on the Elimination of All Forms of Discrimination Against Women (CEDAW), to which Pakistan acceded in 1996, requires the government to take action to eliminate violence against women as a form of discrimination that inhibits women's ability to enjoy rights and freedoms on a basis of equality with men. Pakistan's CEDAW obligations extend to the provision of an effective remedy to women victims of violence. Furthermore, the International Covenant on Civil and Political Rights (ICCPR), which Pakistan has not signed but which is a cornerstone of international human rights law, requires governments to ensure the rights to life and security of the person of all individuals in their jurisdiction, without distinction of any kind, including sex. In line with the ICCPR, Pakistan should not only refrain from, but should also prevent private actors from committing, acts of violence against women. Human Rights Watch found that rather than responding actively to violations of women's rights to life, to security of the person, and to be free of discrimination, the government has acted, through its police, medicolegal, prosecutorial, and judicial systems, to block access to redress and justice for women victims of violence.

II. RECOMMENDATIONS

To the Government of Pakistan

Legislative and Regulatory Reform:
- The Offence of *Zina* Ordinance, which codifies Pakistan's current law on rape and adultery/fornication, does not provide an adequate legal avenue for victims of rape to obtain justice and should be repealed.

The Zina Ordinance discourages rape victims from filing charges by presenting the threat of potential prosecution for adultery. These laws are also seriously flawed because they fail to criminalize marital rape and to establish the crime of statutory rape or sex with or without the consent of a minor. Furthermore, the definition of rape encompassed by the Zina Ordinance is incomplete; the definition of rape should include anal and oral penetration as well as penetration by foreign objects such as sticks, bottles, or knives.

- The former provisions of the Pakistan Penal Code on rape should be re-enacted into law with amendments to make marital rape a criminal offense and to incorporate the broader definition of rape given above.

- Pending repeal of the Zina Ordinance, immediate steps should be taken to ascribe different section numbers to the crimes of zina (adultery/fornication) and zina *bil jabr* (rape).

Currently these crimes are established by Section 10(2) and Section 10(3) of the ordinance respectively. Subsuming both crimes under Section 10 has led to great confusion in the registration of First Information Requests (FIRs) for rape and in subsequent legal proceedings, which are based on the contents of the FIR. The police frequently register rape complaints simply under Section 10 of the Zina Ordinance, without specifying the applicable subsection. The ensuing ambiguity as to the type of crime in question not only mars the police investigation but also leads to additional trauma for the rape victim because of the potential created for a wrongful prosecution for adultery. Furthermore, since amending an FIR is a very difficult process, in most cases the ambiguity persists until final disposition of the case. In a few instances, police sloppiness in registering FIRs has led to rape prosecutions proceeding under Section 10(2) of the Zina Ordinance, which has resulted in lower sentences for defendants. Hence it is imperative that the crime of zina bil jabr be codified under a completely separate and free-standing section of the ordinance.

Recommendations

- Article 151(4) of the *Qanun-e-Shahadat* Order of 1984 that, in cases of rape and attempted rape, allows for the admission of evidence to show that "the prosecutrix was of a generally immoral character" should be repealed; the Qanun-e-Shahadat Order should be amended to prohibit explicitly the admission of such evidence.

It is now widely recognized that the general reputation of the victim has no bearing on whether she was raped in a particular instance. Many countries have enacted "rape shield laws" that explicitly bar the admission of reputation or opinion evidence relating to a woman's past sexual behavior in rape cases. Such rape shield laws also prohibit the admission of other evidence regarding a woman's past sexual behavior outside of a few limited exceptions.

- Article 17 of the Qanun-e-Shahadat Order of 1984 should be amended to explicitly guarantee the right of women to have their testimony given equal weight to that of men in all cases.

- A specific set of laws should be enacted explicitly criminalizing all forms of domestic and familial violence against women, including assault, battery, burns, acid burns, sexual assault, forced abortions, and illegal confinement, at the hands of husbands, in-laws, and other relatives.

- A provision should be added to the Criminal Law (Amendment) Act of 1997 to specify that "honor killings" are punishable as *qatl-e-amd* (intentional murder) and to explicitly prohibit the practice of mitigation of sentences in such cases. There should be an explicit prohibition against the application of the common law defense of grave and sudden provocation to cases of honor killings.

- The Criminal Law (Amendment) Act of 1997 should set out clear guidelines for assessing and distributing *diyat* (blood money or monetary compensation) based on the principle of gender parity and non-discrimination. Hence it should be explicitly stated in the law that the amount of diyat for male and female victims should be equal, to be distributed in equal shares among male and female heirs. Courts should retain discretion to allocate larger shares to heirs who are minors or physically or mentally disabled.

- A provision should be added to the Code of Criminal Procedure to allow judges, at the request of the victim, to hold rape and domestic violence trials *in camera.* Such a provision is necessary in light of the social stigma attached to rape and the psychological trauma experienced by victims of rape and domestic violence, which may be heightened by a public proceeding.

- For the same reasons, and given the consequent reluctance of victims of these crimes to approach the courts, the Code of Criminal Procedure should be amended to empower courts to withold the name, address, and other identifying information about the victim in rape and domestic violence cases from the media and general public.

- The government of Pakistan should sign and ratify, without reservations, and bring domestic law and practice into compliance with, the International Covenant on Civil and Political Rights.

Reform of Police Practice and Rules:
- The police rules should establish clear and explicit guidelines for police intervention in cases of domestic abuse, including standardized arrest policies for perpetrators. Women victims of such violence are entitled to equal protection and enforcement of the law. Family violence cases should not be treated as "private problems" and as therefore unsuitable for intervention by the criminal justice system. It should be made clear that it is inappropriate conduct for the police to attempt to get the concerned parties to reconcile or reach a settlement.

- A standard course of training on domestic violence, rape, and sexual assault should be required for new police recruits and serving officers. The government should commission individuals and organizations with expertise and experience in working with women victims of violence to develop a training program and to achieve its national implementation.

Police must be trained to eliminate gender biases in their responses to cases of violence against women. They should receive basic legal training to enable them to distinguish between crimes of zina (adultery or fornication) and zina bil jabr (rape), comprehend the criminal nature of spousal and other family violence, and understand the parameters and elements of criminal assault. In particular the police should be trained to realize that domestic or family violence is not to be excused, tolerated, or condoned under any circumstances. In addition, the police should be trained in investigative methodology applicable to cases of domestic and sexual violence, including effective and respectful interviewing procedures for victims of these crimes and methods for protecting victims and witnesses from harassment by defendants (including physical violence, threats, and bribes to withdraw complaints). Police should receive professional training in basic medicolegal principles, methods for gathering medical and other forensic evidence, and in the legal and evidentiary significance of medical information in rape cases.

- The police rule requiring that an FIR should be filed immediately upon receiving a complaint should be rigorously enforced, although filing an FIR should not be a prerequisite to obtaining a medicolegal exam for rape victims.

- Women who have been raped or sexually assaulted and report to a police station should be given the option to be taken immediately by the police to be examined by a specialist medicolegal practitioner. In rape cases women should also be able to go directly for a medicolegal examination without police escort or intervention. Hence, in cases of rape, there should be no requirement, in law or in practice, that an official complaint or FIR be registered prior to the victim's medicolegal examination. The requirement of obtaining a magistrate's order prior to the victim's medicolegal examination should also be eliminated in rape cases, provided that medicolegal doctors take the woman's written consent before conducting such exams. In adultery or fornication cases, however, the requirement that an FIR be lodged and a magistrate determine the accused's consent before a medicolegal examination is performed should be maintained.

- The government should create an independent mechanism in each province to monitor and oversee police treatment of women victims of violence. This body should be empowered to hear complaints and to take steps to discipline police officers who reject complaints of sexual or domestic violence without cause, harass complainants or their families, close cases without cause, or accept bribes to block investigations.

- More women's police stations should be established with equivalent status to other police stations. The staff of women's police stations should be equipped and trained to refer women victims of violence to shelters, legal aid organizations, and other nongovernmental organizations offering support services for abuse victims.

The Medicolegal System:

- Rape victims should have access to medicolegal exams performed by female practitioners twenty-four hours a day, seven days a week, including national holidays. The availability of female practitioners should be ensured by having one present on the premises of medicolegal centers at all times. The fact that a female practitioner is technically "on call" does not guarantee that victims will receive timely examinations.

- In large metropolitan centers like Karachi and Lahore, there should be at least two geographically dispersed and fully staffed venues where victims of rape may obtain medicolegal examinations at all times. At present, at any given time, rape victims are examined at only one venue in each city; this poses considerable logistical hurdles to victims who live far removed from the downtown districts. At a minimum, either an additional full-service medicolegal center should be established in each city, or one major government hospital should have a female medicolegal doctor available on the premises twenty-four hours a day to examine victims of rape.

- Women who have been sexually assaulted and report to a public health facility should, wherever possible and with their written consent, be examined for medicolegal purposes at that facility, if necessary after calling a specialist from elsewhere to carry out the examination. The woman should be informed of her right to lay a charge and, with her consent, police should be called to the facility for the crime to be reported. Police involvement should not, however, be a prerequisite for conducting the medicolegal examination, which should always be carried out as soon as possible.

- The services rendered by medicolegal doctors at the specialized medicolegal centers should be expanded beyond collection of medical evidence to the provision of basic medical treatment and referrals to nongovernmental organizations providing legal aid and counseling to victims of sexual and other violence.

Recommendations 11

- More female medicolegal doctors should be appointed in both urban and rural areas.

- Explicit regulations should be adopted to allow private doctors to be certified to conduct, in rape cases, official medical exams that would constitute admissible evidence at trial.

- The nature of the medicolegal examination performed on victims of rape and sexual assault and the format of the medicolegal report in such cases should be immediately changed. The focus of the exam should be on detecting signs of *nonconsensual* sexual intercourse rather than attempting to check the purported virginity status and vaginal elasticity of the examinee. The victim's entire body should be thoroughly examined for signs of struggle and for foreign materials of forensic significance, such as clothing fibers, twigs, sand, and gravel. The medicolegal report should make no reference to the examinee's presumed level of sexual activity based on the "finger test" or any ostensible assessment of her vaginal elasticity. Such notations on the medicolegal report have no legitimate probative value in a rape case and are highly prejudicial and inflammatory, as well as being medically baseless.

- The medicolegal examination performed on women accused of zina should also focus on detecting signs of nonconsensual sexual intercourse, since, in many cases, women who have been raped are falsely accused of zina. The practice of checking the virginity status of women accused of zina should be discontinued in light of the scientifically flawed methods employed for this purpose. Modern medical standards hold that the use of the condition of the hymen to indicate recent sexual intercourse or virginity status is medically groundless.

- The medicolegal examinations performed on suspected rapists should not be limited to a potency test. The suspect's body should also be examined for signs of struggle, such as scratch marks and bruises.

- Training programs should be developed and systematically implemented for all government doctors entrusted with medicolegal duties in rape and adultery/fornication cases, both as a requirement before appointment and as annual in-service training. These programs should focus on relevant medicolegal methodology and principles, the psychological impact of sexual assault on victims, and the legal significance of medical evidence in these cases. Doctors should be trained in methods to present their findings effectively and professionally in court.

- Manuals should be developed for doctors responsible for examining rape victims that outline the relevant laws for their work, review specialized medicolegal techniques (for example, ways of determining the time of injury), and provide detailed descriptions of injuries specific to sexual assault in both adult and child victims.

- Standardized protocols for the examination and treatment of victims of rape and the collection of biological samples should be developed and distributed to all those engaged in conducting medicolegal examinations in rape cases.

- All government medical facilities where medicolegal exams are conducted should be adequately supplied and maintained to ensure the performance of effective and hygienic examinations.

- Governmental laboratories where medicolegal samples are analyzed should be adequately staffed, supplied, and supervised, so they can provide fast, reliable, and professional service. The two main laboratories, the Offices of the Chemical Examiner in Karachi and Lahore, and all secondary goverment laboratories under the supervision of these offices, should be strictly monitored by the relevant provincial health departments to identify corrupt and inefficient practices.

- Provincial departments of health should develop and implement training programs for laboratory staff, both as a requirement before appointment and as annual in-service training.

- The provincial departments of health should set and strictly enforce an appropriate timeline during which the Offices of the Chemical Examiner in their respective jurisdictions must complete testing samples and send out the results. At present the Offices of the Chemical Examiner observe no systematic timelines for conducting standard tests on medicolegal samples and frequently inordinately delay isssuing analysis reports, at times seriously hindering the progress of rape trials.

Recommendations

Improved Prosecution Services:

- Special prosecutors should be identified in every district to try cases of rape and other forms of violence against women. These prosecutors should not be assigned to the court of a particular judge but should be empowered to handle cases of violence against women in all the trial courts in their district.

- Prosecutors responsible for cases of violence against women should be trained to eliminate gender bias in their approach to and handling of these cases and to recognize the serious and criminal nature of domestic violence. In addition, prosecutors should receive specialized training in prosecuting sexual assault trials, which must impart an understanding of legal theories applicable in rape cases and a thorough grasp of the legal significance and courtroom use of medicolegal evidence.

- Prosecutors should be instructed to argue for the imposition of strict bail conditions in cases of family violence in which there is a history of violent assault.

Victim Services:

- The government should give top priority to the provision of shelters for abused women and their dependent children, with the assistance of nongovernmental organizations with experience working with women victims of violence and knowledgeable about their needs. Seeking residence at such shelters should be a strictly voluntary option for women. Shelters should *not* function as remand homes or serve any custodial or reformatory purpose. In addition, the government should fund programs to provide legal assistance and counseling services for women at the shelters.

- The government should help fund telephone hotlines for women victims of violence in all major cities. These hotlines should be widely publicized and operated by trained staff who can offer basic counseling and refer women to specialized service providers and to shelters.

- More burn units should be established in government hospitals. The capacity of existing burn units should also be expanded and the quality of care should be improved.

- Efforts to monitor and improve the Pakistan government's response to violence against women would be greatly enhanced by the availability of reliable national statistics detailing the nature and degree of such violence, the rates of prosecution and conviction, and the nature of punishment applicable in cases of sexual assault and other violence against women. At present, statistics regarding adultery/fornication and rape are commingled. It is imperative that rape be identified as an independent crime category for which separate statistics are compiled. Similarly, domestic violence cases should be distinguished from other assaults, and comprehensive statistics about the incidence of domestic violence and about court proceedings initiated in such cases should be recorded and disseminated.

Recommendations to the United Nations

- The Secretary-General of the United Nations and the United Nations High Commissioner on Human Rights should ensure that all United Nations agencies operating in Pakistan pay particular attention to the issue of violence against women and develop programs and strategies designed to curb that abuse and promote accountability.

- The United Nations Committee on the Elimination of Discrimination Against Women should take note of the Pakistan government's inadequate response to the problem of violence against women and press the United Nations Human Rights Commission to examine the government of Pakistan's compliance with applicable international laws and standards outlawing discrimination against women.

- The World Health Organization (WHO) should provide technical assistance to the government of Pakistan in developing standardized protocols for conducting medicolegal examinations in cases of rape and sexual assault and in identifying effective medicolegal techniques and requisite equipment to implement the protocols. WHO should also assist the government of Pakistan in designing and implementing training programs for medicolegal doctors responsible for conducting these medicolegal examinations.

- The United Nations Development Programme, in conjunction with the Pakistan government and nongovernmental organizations, should design and implement service programs for women victims of sexual and other violence, inlcuding legal literacy, legal aid, counseling, shelter, and job training programs.

Recommendations to the World Bank and Other International Lending Institutions

Given its relationship with the Pakistan government, and its priority on working with NGOs in Pakistan, the World Bank is in a particularly influential position to promote constructive reforms and to assist in meeting the needs of women victims of violence.

- In its ongoing policy dialogue with the government on gender issues, the bank should urge improvements in the legal infrastructure and other reforms that would help address some of the fundamental obstacles to women seeking redress for crimes of sexual and domestic violence.

- Assisting the Pakistan government in developing an effective policy on sexual and domestic violence, in compliance with its international treaty commitments, should be an explicit objective included in the Country Assistance Strategy (CAS) when it is adopted by the bank to lay out a framework for its development work over the following three years. Progress on gender equity and sustainable development for women in Pakistan cannot take place in an environment in which women's basic rights are routinely violated by a system that does not protect them from sexual and domestic violence. Bilateral donors participating in the next consultative group (CG) annual donor meeting, convened by the World Bank, should also raise these concerns at the CG.

- With its NGO partners in Pakistan and government authorities at the national, provincial, and local levels, the bank should explore possibilities for pilot projects aimed at assisting both rural and urban women, including the establishment and funding of medicolegal clinics set up specifically to meet the needs of women subject to violence. The bank should also do an assessment study, with NGO input, of the need for women's shelters and offer to fund the establishment of shelters.

- International lending institutions should make it a priority to provide funds for programs with nongovernmental organizations and the Pakistan government to train police, prosecutors, and judges to eliminate gender bias in dealing with cases of rape, sexual assault, and spousal battery and to treat these cases with the requisite seriousness and rigor.

- International lending institutions should make it a priority to provide funds to the Pakistan government for improving its medicolegal services. Funds should be earmarked for training personnel as well as upgrading physical facilities and equipment.

- International lending institutions should make it a priority to provide funds to nongovernmental organizations and the Pakistan government for the provision of basic services for women victims of violence, including legal aid, medical care, and counseling.

- International lending institutions should, prior to approval of projects, investigate the effect of proposed policies and programs on the welfare and status of women. Projects with adverse discriminatory consequences for women should not be pursued.

Recommendations to the International Community

Bilateral donors, including Japan, the European Union, and the United States should

- Use their influence to encourage Pakistan to adopt the recommendations outlined above. They should raise the issue of an inadequate government response to the problem of violence against women at every diplomatic opportunity at high levels and through their embassies in Pakistan.

- Grant funds for and design, in cooperation with nongovernmental organizations, programs to provide basic services for women victims of violence. These services should include women's shelters, medical care, counseling, and legal aid, which are necessary to encourage and enable women to come forward and seek safety from and justice for abusive treatment.

Recommendations

- Encourage Pakistan to repeal the discriminatory Zina Ordinance and to reenact Pakistan's previous rape laws with an amendment to make marital rape a criminal offense.

- Use their influence to encourage Pakistan to implement specific legislation that would explicitly criminalize domestic violence.

- Provide funds to the Pakistan government for improving its medicolegal services. Funds should be earmarked for training personnel as well as upgrading physical facilities and equipment.

- Organize and fund programs to train police, prosecutors, medicolegal doctors, and judges to eliminate gender bias in handling cases of violence against women.

- Through their "women and development" and "grassroots" initiatives, provide funds for nongovernmental organizations in Pakistan that assist women victims of violence.

- Encourage Pakistan to implement the recommendations of the Commission of Inquiry for Women. The commission was set up through a Senate resolution in September 1994 and presented its report to Prime Minister Nawaz Sharif on August 21, 1997. As this report went to print, the government had not debated, let alone adopted, any of the commission's recommendations.

III. BACKGROUND

The situation of women in Pakistan varies considerably depending on geographical location and class. Women fare better in urban areas and middle- and upper-class sections of society, where there are greater opportunities for higher education and for paid and professional work and women's social mobility is somewhat less restricted.[1] Seventy-five percent of Pakistan's female population is, however, rural,[2] and the average Pakistani woman is beset with the "crippling handicaps of illiteracy, constant motherhood and poor health."[3] And, despite the relative privilege of some, all Pakistani women remain structurally disadvantaged and second-class citizens as a result of legal and societal discrimination premised on social and cultural norms and attitudes.

Women's legal and social status has changed throughout the country's turbulent political history, sometimes for the better, lately for the worse. In 1947 British India was partitioned along religious lines to create two independent nations: India, which had a majority Hindu population, and Pakistan, which was predominantly Muslim. Continuing controversy over the role of Islam in the nation's political life, along with tension among the country's ethnic groups, has dominated the process of state-building in Pakistan since independence. Pakistan's relations with its neighbors, above all Afghanistan and India, have also had critical consequences for foreign and domestic politics, particularly with respect to the role of the military and the course of Islamization. The direction of the debate over the

---

[1] In the less populated frontier provinces of Pakistan, life for women is very restricted, and women are expected to comply with tribal beliefs and traditions. Any woman who deviates from these traditions, such as being seen with a man to whom she is not related or married, can suffer severe penalties, including death. The women observe strict *purdah* (seclusion of women) and are rarely seen outside their homes. However, in the more heavily populated provinces of Sindh and Punjab, which account for well over half of Pakistan's population, women have relatively greater social mobility. They are visible, working in the fields or in village areas, and have increased access to education and health care. Women in Pakistan's urban centers, although a small minority of the total female population, have the greatest mobility, with considerable access to jobs and education and greater freedom in marriage and divorce.

[2] Ayesha Jalal, "The Convenience of Subservience: Women and the State in Pakistan," Deniz Kandiyoti, ed., *Women, Islam and the State* (Philadelphia, PA: Temple University Press, 1991), p. 77.

[3] Government of Pakistan, *The Sixth Five Year Plan 1988-1993 and Prospective Plan 1988-2003*, (Islamabad, 1988).

country's political ideology and the militarization of politics have had a profound impact on the trajectory of women's advancement.

The constitutional debates following partition were dominated by protracted arguments over the place of the *shari`a,* or Islamic legal principles, in Pakistani law. While Pakistan's *ulama*[4] argued that the shari`a provided the only legitimate basis for the new state, most politicians fought for a constitution that embodied the principles of modern parliamentary democracy. The debates lasted nine years and ultimately produced a constitution that "demonstrated . . . [an] unwillingness to articulate and implement an Islamic ideology" in that the "relationship of modern constitutional concepts to Islamic principles was asserted but not delineated."[5]

Still, Pakistan's early leaders gave in to some of the demands of the religious leadership by including in the Constitution the declaration that Pakistan was an Islamic republic and by granting the ulama an advisory role, though it carried little influence.[6] But if there was little confidence in Islam as the basis for building political consensus, there was equally little faith in the country's weak political institutions.[7] As a result, the military came to assume a dominant role in Pakistani politics. The intervention of the military in politics eventually led, during the martial law administration of General Zia-ul-Haq, to disastrous consequences for the advancement of women's rights.

General Zia ul-Haq, then Army chief of staff, overthrew the elected government of Zulfiqar Ali Bhutto in a military coup in July 1977. A beleaguered Bhutto had himself set the stage for his downfall by imposing martial law during a period of widespread civil unrest following a national election held in March of that year. In that election, Bhutto's party, the Pakistan People's Party (PPP), faced a formidable challenge from the Pakistan National Alliance, a coalition that

---

[4] Scholars of Islamic law, generally considered the most powerful religious authorities in Islam. The singular is *alim.*

[5] John Esposito, "Islam: Ideology and Politics in Pakistan," in Ali Banuazizi and Myron Weiner, eds., *The State, Religion and Ethnic Politics* (Syracuse, NY: Syracuse University Press, 1986), p. 336.

[6] It is possible they feared the ulama might attempt to provoke communal disturbances. Khawar Mumtaz and Farida Shaheed, "Women of Pakistan," *Two Steps Forward, One Step Back* (London: Zed Books, Ltd., 1987), p. 7.

[7] According to Stephen Cohen, the early political parties in Pakistan did not really operate as channels for group demands or instruments of state policy but instead often functioned as vehicles for local feudal leaders. Stephen P. Cohen, "State Building in Pakistan," in Banuazizi and Weiner, *The State, Religion and Ethnic Politics* (Syracuse, NY: Syracuse University Press, 1986), pp. 306-307.

included the entire opposition from fundamentalist religious to centrist and liberal parties. In an effort to boost his popularity, Bhutto had made some moves to win over the religious establishment.[8] Although these moves anticipated Zia's later Islamization programs, they failed to win Bhutto much support among religious leaders, who denounced his avowed socialism. Bhutto also alienated the left, which joined the opposition alliance, along with urban middle-class Pakistanis frustrated with Bhutto's increasingly autocratic and repressive rule[9] and failure to implement economic reforms. Although the PPP officially won the election by a large margin, the opposition claimed extensive electoral fraud and immediately began the anti-government agitation that resulted in the imposition of martial law, which led to Bhutto's ouster.

Zia's coup represented the convergence of conservative religious interests with those of the army. In the absence of any clear popular constituency, Zia used appeals to Islamic values to legitimize his regime and cultivated the support of the conservative religious parties. In return, he provided those parties, which had never had strong support from the electorate, with access to national political power. Zia came to power denouncing Bhutto's administration as un-Islamic, and one of his main rallying cries was the return of Pakistani society to the "moral purity of early Islam." His most vulnerable and strategic targets, along with minorities, were women, whom he promised to return to the sanctity of the *chardivari* (the four walls of the home), thus reaffirming women's domestic role as the cornerstone of a Muslim way of life.

The fact that women's status became a lightning rod in Zia's political strategy came as no surprise. Women had historically been used to stabilize the unsteady balance between religion and politics in Pakistan. Within months of taking power, Zia introduced a series of legal and social changes that reversed many of the legal advances for women of the prior thirty years. This backsliding demonstrated that, despite seeming progress, women's rights ultimately remained

---

[8] Bhutto's most significant step, in his bid to court support from religious leaders, was the 1974 amendment to the Constitution that declared the minority Ahmadi sect non-Muslims. He also introduced symbolic measures, such as banning liquor sales and recognizing Friday instead of Sunday as the official weekly holiday.

[9] According to Amnesty International, before the March 1977 elections there were several thousand political prisoners in jail in Pakistan, most of whom had been held without trial. Thousands more were arrested in the days before and after the election. Special tribunals set up to try political detainees suspended ordinary rights of due process and police engaged in torture and intimidation to extract confessions. *See* Amnesty International, *Report 1977* (London: Amnesty International, 1977), pp. 202-8.

tentative and discretionary. Women's few hard-won legal gains were quickly curtailed.

With the imposition of martial law, Zia suspended all fundamental rights guaranteed in the Constitution that had been adopted in 1973, including the right to be free of discrimination on the basis of sex. He then introduced a series of laws that gave legal sanction to women's subordinate status, including the *Hudood* Ordinances, which changed the law of rape and adultery and made fornication a crime for the first time in the country's history; and the *Qanun-e-Shahadat* Order (Law of Evidence Order), which relegates women to inferior legal status and, in some circumstances, renders the testimony of a woman equal to only half the weight of a man's. Zia also proposed laws regarding *Qisas* and *Diyat*, Islamic penal laws governing compensation and retribution in crimes involving bodily injury. (These laws and their discriminatory effects are discussed in greater detail in the next section of this report.) Zia reinforced the legal strictures he imposed on women with a series of informal regulations and unwritten policies designed to curtail women's personal liberty, visibility, and participation in public life.

Zia's Islamization efforts had their greatest impact on Pakistan's criminal justice system. The potential for misuse of power by the police and jail authorities had existed since colonial times, and successive periods of martial law had further increased the powers of law enforcement agencies and eroded safeguards against abuses. Far from providing better protection for people with legitimate grievances, the effect of Islamization was to increase the state's power over the lives and liberties of its citizens, bringing more of them, particularly women, into contact with an already abusive and corrupt criminal justice system. Zia also undermined the independence of the civilian court system with, among other things, the introduction at the High Court level of *shariat* benches, reorganized and centralized as the Federal Shariat Court (FSC) in 1980,[10] to review all laws to ensure that none

---

[10] The Federal Shariat Court's jurisdiction exceeds that of the High Courts because it alone has "revisional" powers. It can, either on its own or in response to a citizen's petition, review any provision of Pakistani law to determine "whether or not any law or provision of law is repugnant to the Injunctions of Islam, as contained in the Holy Quran and Sunnah of the Holy Prophet." Constitution of Pakistan, Part VII, Article 203D(1). If it finds the law repugnant, the FSC can declare the law invalid and force the legislature either to amend it or let it lapse. In addition, the FSC can change any finding or sentence in any case decided under the Hudood laws. This includes the ability to change an acquittal to a conviction without risking double jeopardy. (Double jeopardy is the term for the prohibition against trying someone twice for the same crime.) Constitution of Pakistan, Part VII, Article 203(D). This arrangement, in effect, gives the FSC sweeping and barely reviewable revisional powers. These include the power of self-review. The FSC has the

was repugnant to the Koran or the *Sunnah* (exemplary sayings and directives of the prophet Mohammed) and to hear appeals in certain criminal matters including Hudood cases.[11]

The Zia era produced a decided shift in the uneasy balance between women's rights and religion in Pakistani politics. Until 1977 the constantly changing religious and political alignments worked against both conservative and progressive extremes, and, with the help of a growing number of independent organizations, women were able to secure a steady flow of moderate reforms, although their impact on the majority of women was minimal. After Zia's coup, the politics of the army and the religious right were so closely aligned that the opportunity for reform disappeared, and women took a step backward. Increased social control of women was an important part of the Zia regime's appropriation of conservative religious values to legitimate state power.

This is not to say that there was no opposition to Zia's policies toward women. In September 1981, women came together in Karachi in an emergency meeting to oppose the adverse effects on women of martial law and the Islamization campaign. They launched what was to become the first full-fledged national women's movement in Pakistan: the Women's Action Forum (WAF). Staging public protests and campaigns against the Hudood Ordinances, the Law of Evidence, and the Qisas and Diyat laws (temporarily shelved as a result), WAF became one of the main voices of opposition to Zia.

The coming to power in 1988 of Benazir Bhutto, daughter of Zulfiqar Ali Bhutto, represented an unprecedented alignment of state power with an apparently progressive women's rights policy. However, soon after Bhutto's election, it became clear that, once again, the protection of women's rights had been subordinated to the need to maintain a delicate balance between various political forces, including those representing conservative religious values. Although Bhutto's campaign pledge to repeal the Hudood laws and to remove all other discriminatory statutes had great appeal, her promises on women's rights gradually

---

legal authority to alter its own decisions. Constitution of Pakistan, Part VII, Article 203E(9). This power has provided an incentive to the government to try to influence it. The FSC's decisions are binding on all High Courts and thus on all of the courts that are subordinate to the High Courts. Constitution of Pakistan, Part VII, Article 203G. The High Courts' decisions are binding only on the lower courts. Constitution of Pakistan, Part VII, Article 201. Appeals from the High Courts and the FSC in criminal cases may be taken to the Supreme Court.

[11] Appeals from Hudood criminal convictions resulting in sentences greater than two years' imprisonment are the exclusive province of the FSC.

proved to be empty. During her two incomplete terms in office, she did not repeal a single one of Zia's Islamization laws.[12] The appointment, through elections in 1997, of Prime Minister Nawaz Sharif, appears to have blocked all opportunities for the advancement of women's rights. Sharif, a political protégé of Zia's, had also held office for a truncated term (1990-1993) between Ms. Bhutto's two terms (1988-90 and 1993-96). His actions during during both periods at the helm indicate a political strategy of Islamization akin to his mentor's, with detrimental consequences for women. When he first came to power in November 1990, Sharif promised to adopt Islamic law as the supreme law of Pakistan, albeit within a constitutional framework, and in April 1991 he introduced legislation to that effect. Furthermore, in 1997 Sharif and his supporters in parliament enacted the Qisas and Diyat Ordinance—which institutes shari`a-based changes in Pakistan's criminal law—into law, making it a permanent part of the Pakistan Penal Code rather than an ordinance subject to periodic renewal.

Since his party's return to power in 1997, Nawaz Sharif has moved to consolidate his power by undercutting human rights protections and attacking the supremacy of the Constitution. He has proposed a fifteenth amendment to the Constitution that would entirely replace the existing legal system with a comprehensive Islamic one and would override the "constitution and any law or judgment of any court."[13] Introducing his proposal, Sharif told parliament, "Simple changes in laws are not enough. I want to implement complete Islamic laws where the Koran and Sunnat are supreme."[14] The proposal was quickly approved in the National Assembly (lower house), where Sharif's party has a commanding majority, but, as of July 1999, remained stalled in the Senate and continued to face strong opposition from women's groups, human rights activists, and opposition political parties.[15]

Nawaz Sharif's continuing Islamization efforts have not only reinforced the legitimacy of Zia ul-Haq's discriminatory Islamic laws; they have in effect also bestowed greater discretion and authority on judges to give legal weight, by invoking Islamic precedents and references at random, to biased assumptions about women in a variety of civil and criminal cases. For example, since 1996 courts have admitted cases challenging an adult woman's right to marry of her own free

---

[12] Her promise to do so was made especially difficult to fulfill due to the fact that, by virtue of the eighth consitutional amendment imposed by Zia, these laws were protected both from ordinary legislative modification and from judicial review.

[13] Associated Press, "Pakistan Moves Closer to Islamic Rule," October 9, 1998.

[14] Associated Press, "Pakistan Proposes New Islamic Laws," August 28, 1998.

[15] Associated Press, "Pakistan Moves Closer to Islamic Rule," October 9, 1998.

will, ostensibly an established right under family laws. Judges have looked to the Koran to settle the question, in some cases holding that a Muslim woman's marriage is illegal without familial consent. A 1997 ruling by the Lahore High Court, in the highly publicized Saima Waheed case, upheld a woman's right to marry freely but called for amendments to the family laws, on the basis of Islamic norms, to enforce parental authority to discourage "love marriages."

Women, as a daily practical matter, are far outside the mainstream of political life; a coherent program of concrete measures and a deliberate reversal of existing government attitudes and policies are required to change their situation. Women's access to health and education is severely limited, and their levels of economic and political participation are very low. The literacy rate for Pakistani women is only 25 percent; the maternal mortality rate is disturbingly high at 600 per 100,000 births.[16] Prevailing trends in the health and education sectors are not encouraging. According to one study, "Health and education (especially for women) have been consistently receiving diminishing allocations in the budget (among the lowest in the third world) and much of what is to be distributed disappears through institutionalized corruption. . . Reproductive health services have particularly suffered and are available only where a few major NGOs have outreach, but they cover only a tiny fraction of the population."[17] Women's participation in the economic arena is disproportionately low, with women constituting only 28 percent of the country's labor force,[18] and their marginal role in civic and political life is reflected by the fact that there are only seven female members of the federal parliament, five in the National Assembly out of a total of 207 (2.4 percent) and two in the Senate out of of eighty-three (2.4 percent); one woman among 483 male members of the four provincial legislatures (0.2 percent);[19] two women Cabinet ministers; and three women judges in the provincial High Courts.[20] Not surprisingly, in 1997 Pakistan slid back to 120th out of 146

---

[16] World Bank, *World Development Indicators, 1997* (Washington, D.C.: World Bank, 1997).

[17] Women's Environment and Development Organization, *Mapping Progress: Assessing Implementation of the Beijing Platform, 1998*, (New York: Women's Environment and Development Organization, 1998).

[18] World Bank, *World Development Indicators, 1997* (Washington, D.C.: World Bank, 1997).

[19] Cited in Amnesty International, *Pakistan: No Progress on Women's Rights*, (London: Amnesty International, 1998), p. 2.

[20] Women's Environment and Development Organization, *Mapping Progress: Assessing Implementation of the Beijing Platform, 1998*, (New York: Women's Environment and Development Organization, 1998).

places in the United Nations Development Programme's gender-related development index (107 out of 137 in 1996) and occupied the ninety-second of ninety-four places with regard to women's progressive empowerment.[21]

Clear violations of international law on the rights of women occur daily in Pakistan. Laws that discriminate against women remain on the books and are actively enforced, discrimination in access to government resources and services continues unchecked, and discriminatory practices go unpunished. In particular, violence against women remains a serious and widespread problem—to which the government responds with inaction and inertia. The remainder of this report focuses on the barriers to justice that women victims of violence confront in Pakistan.

---

[21] Cited in Amnesty International, *Pakistan: No Progress on Women's Rights*, (London: Amnesty International, 1998), p. 1.

IV. PAKISTAN'S OBLIGATIONS UNDER INTERNATIONAL LAW

Through its ratification of the U.N. Convention on the Elimination of All Forms of Discrimination against Women (CEDAW)[22] in 1996, Pakistan assumed the obligation to protect women from sexual and other forms of gender-based violence perpetrated by state agents and private actors alike. As a party to CEDAW, Pakistan is obliged "to pursue by all appropriate means and without delay a policy of eliminating discrimination against women"[23] including "any distinction, exclusion or restriction made on the basis of sex which has the purpose of impairing or nullifying the recognition, enjoyment or exercise by women . . . on a basis of equality of men or women, of human rights and fundamental freedoms. . . ."[24] The U.N. Committee on the Elimination of Discrimination Against Women (CEDAW Comittee), established under CEDAW, has noted that "[g]ender-based violence is a form of discrimination which seriously inhibits women's ability to enjoy rights and freedoms on a basis of equality with men."[25] As part of its obligation to prevent violence against women as a step toward eliminating sex discrimination, the government is required to ensure that women victims of violence have access to an effective remedy for the violation of their rights.[26] This duty to provide an effective remedy requires the government to show due diligence in investigating and prosecuting instances of violence against women.[27] In such cases, the effective collection of medical evidence is an integral part of a proper investigation, which, in turn, is central to the successful implementation of penal sanctions against perpetrators of violence against women. Similarly, the ability of the police, prosecutors, and judges to evaluate and use medical evidence is critical to ensuring effective prosecutions of perpetrators of violence against women. Hence, pursuant to its legal obligations under CEDAW, the government of Pakistan

---

[22] Adopted and opened for signature, ratification, and accession by General Assembly resolution 34/180 of December 18, 1979; entry into force September 3, 1981. Pakistan ratified CEDAW on December 3, 1996.

[23] CEDAW Article 2.

[24] CEDAW Article 1.

[25] Committee on the Elimination of Discrimination against Women, "Violence Against Women," General Recommendation No. 19 (Eleventh session, 1992), (New York: United Nations),CEDAW/C 1992/L.1/Add.15, para. 1.

[26] CEDAW obligates states to "establish legal protection of the rights of women on an equal basis with men and to ensure through competent national tribunals and other public institutions the effective protection of women against any act of discrimination." Article 2.

[27] CEDAW Article 2.

must provide an efficient and effective system of collection of medical evidence to facilitate the proper investigation and prosecution of cases of violence against women. Toward the same end, the state must ensure that the police, prosecutors, and judges are fully trained and prepared to interpret and utilize medical evidence in order to advance the prosecution of violence against women without prejudice to the accused.

In 1992 the CEDAW Committee adopted a general recommendation and comments on states' obligations under CEDAW that spelled out the facets of any potentially effective remedy to the problem of violence against women. The committee noted that states are obliged under CEDAW to take steps to provide the following:

> (a) Effective legal measures, including penal sanctions, civil remedies and compensatory provisions to protect women against all kinds of violence, including *inter alia* violence and abuse in the family, sexual assault and sexual harassment in the workplace;
> (b) Preventive measures, including public information and education programmes to change attitudes concerning the roles and status of men and women;
> (c) Protective measures, including refuges, counseling, rehabilitation and support services for women who are the victims of violence or who are at risk of violence.[28]

The duties enumerated by the CEDAW Committee extend beyond the criminal justice system and encompass preventive and protective measures, including "refuges, counseling, rehabilitation and support services."[29] The U.N. Declaration of Basic Principles of Justice for Victims of Crime and Abuse of Power[30] similarly provides that "[v]ictims should receive the necessary material, medical, psychological and social assistance through governmental, voluntary, community-based and indigenous means."[31] In accordance with these recognized standards, the state should take affirmative measures to promote women's access

---

[28] Committee on the Elimination of Discrimination Against Women, "Violence Against Women," General Recommendation No. 19 (Eleventh session, 1992), U.N. Document CEDAW/C/1992/L.1/Add.15.
[29] Ibid.
[30] Adopted by U.N. General Assembly resolution 40/34 of November 29, 1985.
[31] Principle 14.

to health care services, including psychological care. The state should also establish immediately quality shelters for battered women that function not as de facto detention facilities but as refuges where women can find safety and shelter without compromising their personal autonomy and freedom of movement.

In its Declaration on the Elimination of Violence Against Women, adopted in December 1993, the United Nations reaffirmed the state's obligation of due diligence, especially as it applies to the protection of women from violence.[32] The declaration denounces violence against women, including violence in the home, as "a violation of the rights and fundamental freedoms of women."[33] It provides that "states should condemn violence against women . . . [and] exercise due diligence to prevent, investigate, and in accordance with national legislation, punish acts of violence against women."[34] The declaration explicitly states that governments' obligation applies regardless of "whether those acts [of violence] are perpetuated by the State or by private persons."[35]

Furthermore, the International Covenant on Civil and Political Rights (ICCPR), which Pakistan has not ratified but is a cornerstone of international human rights law, requires governments to ensure the rights to life and security of the person of all individuals in their jurisdiction, without distinction of any kind, including sex.[36] The ICCPR would require Pakistan to not only refrain from, but also prevent private actors from committing, acts of violence against women.[37]

---

[32] Declaration on the Elimination of Violence Against Women, February 23, 1994 (New York: United Nations, 1994) A/Res/48/104. This declaration is a non-binding resolution that establishes an international standard.

[33] Ibid., preamble.

[34] Ibid., Art. 4(c).

[35] Ibid.

[36] Arts. 2, 6 and 9.

[37] For additional discussion of international obligations with respect to violence against women by private actors, see Dorothy Q. Thomas and Michele Beasley, "Domestic Violence as a Human Rights Issue," Human Rights Quarterly, vol. 15, no. 1 (February 1993) and Human Rights Watch, *Global Report on Women's Human Rights* (New York: Human Rights Watch, 1995), pp. 39-44.

V. THE SCOPE OF THE PROBLEM OF VIOLENCE AGAINST WOMEN

Women in Pakistan face the threat of multiple forms of violence, including sexual violence by family members, strangers, and state agents; domestic abuse, including spousal murder and being burned, disfigured with acid, beaten, and threatened; ritual honor killings; and custodial abuse and torture. In its annual report for 1997, the nongovernmental Human Rights Commission of Pakistan (HRCP) reported,"The worst victims were women of the poor and middle classes. Their resourcelessness not only made them the primary target of the police and the criminals, it also rendered them more vulnerable to oppressive customs and mores inside homes and outside."[38]

The most endemic form of violence faced by women is violence in the home.[39] For 1997, HRCP reported that "[d]omestic violence remained a pervasive phenomenon. The supremacy of the male and subordination of the female assumed to be part of the culture and even to have sanction of the religion made violence by one against the other in a variety of its forms an accepted and pervasive feature of domestic life."[40] A United Nations report on women echoes this point, explaining the nature of domestic violence generally in terms of the structure of the family:

> Comprehensive studies on domestic violence indicate that domestic violence is a structural rather than causal problem. It is the structure of the family that leads to or legitimizes the acts, emotions or phenomenon that are identified as the "causes" of domestic violence under the causal analysis. This family structure is a "structure that is mirrored and confirmed in the structure of society, which condones the oppression of women and tolerates male violence as one of the instruments in the perpetuation of this power balance."[41]

---

[38] Human Rights Commission of Pakistan, *State of Human Rights in 1996*, (Lahore: Human Rights Commission of Pakistan, 1997), p. 184.

[39] Human Rights Commission of Pakistan, *State of Human Rights in 1997*, p. 130.

[40] Human Rights Commission of Pakistan, *State of Human Rights in 1997*, p. 185.

[41] *Report of the World Conference of the United Nations Decade for Women: Equality, Development and Peace*, Copenhagen, 14-30 July 1980 (UN Publication, Sales No. E.80.IV.3 and Corrigendum), p. 30, cited in Yasmine Hassan, *The Haven Becomes Hell* (Lahore: Shirkat Gah, 1995), p. 6.

Estimates of the percentage of women who experience domestic violence in Pakistan range from 70 to upwards of 90 percent.[42] According to HRCP, "[T]he extreme forms it took included driving a woman to suicide or engineering an 'accident' (frequently the bursting of a kitchen stove) to cause her death . . . usually . . . when the husband, often in collaboration with his side of the family, felt that the dower or other gifts he had expected from his in-laws in consequence of the marriage were not forthcoming, or/and he wanted to marry again, or he expected an inheritance from the death of his wife."[43] During 1997, the Lahore press reported an average of more than four local cases of women being burnt weekly, three of the four fatally.[44] Police follow-up on these cases was negligible, with only six suspects taken into custody out of the 215 cases reported in Lahore newspapers during the year.[45] In 1997, there was not a single conviction in a "stove-death" case in the country.[46] The Lahore press also reported 265 homicides against women in the local area resulting from other forms of intrafamily violence. In the majority of cases, husbands and in-laws were responsible for the murders, while in other cases the perpetrators were brothers and fathers.[47]

Honor killings are another recurrent form of familial violence against women, and again the perpetrators continue to find vindication in the eyes of both the law and society. The practice of summary killing of a woman suspected of an illicit liaison, known as *karo kari* in Sindh and Balochistan, is known to occur in all parts of the country.[48] The Sindh government has reported an annual figure of 300 for such killings.[49] HRCP's own findings reveal that in 1997 there were

---

[42] HRCP as well as an informal study conducted by the Women's Ministry concluded that at least 80 percent of all women in Pakistan are subjected to domestic violence. Human Rights Commission of Pakistan, *State of Human Rights in 1996*, p. 130; Women's Ministry, *Battered Housewives in Pakistan* (Islamabad: Women's Ministry, 1985). Amnesty International has reported that some 95 percent of women are believed to be subjected to such violence. Amnesty International, *Women's Human Rights Remain a Dead Letter* (London: Amnesty International, 1997), ASA 33/07/97. Amnesty International has also reported findings by women's groups in Pakistan that 70 percent of women are subjected to violence in their homes. Amnesty International, *Pakistan: No Progress on Women's Rights* (London: Amnesty International, 1998), ASA 33/13/98.

[43] Human Rights Commission of Pakistan, *State of Human Rights in 1997*, p. 185.
[44] Ibid.
[45] Ibid.
[46] Ibid.
[47] Ibid., p. 186.
[48] Human Rights Commission of Pakistan, *State of Human Rights in 1997*, p. 187.
[49] Ibid.

eighty-six karo kari killings in Larkana, Sindh, alone, with fifty-three of the victims being women.[50]

Sexual assault is also alarmingly common in Pakistan. HRCP estimated that in 1997 at least eight women, more than half of them minors, were raped every twenty-four hours nationwide.[51] The high incidence of sexual assault in the country is partly fostered by the societal subordination of women to men, by the custom of avenging oneself upon one's enemies by raping their women, who are seen as repositories of family honor, and by the impunity with which these crimes are carried out.

There is no question that violence against women is an enormous problem in Pakistan that is exacerbated and perpetuated by the government's inadequate response to the problem. In fact, the state's response to domestic violence in Pakistan is so minimal and cases of intrafamily violence are so rarely addressed in any way by the criminal justice system that it was not possible for us to achieve one of our research goals for this report: that is, to track specific domestic violence criminal suits in order to identify larger patterns in the prosecution of domestic violence. We found that despite the staggering levels of intrafamily violence against women, it is widely perceived by the law enforcement system and society at large as a private family matter, not subject to government intervention let alone criminal sanction. At present there is virtually no prosecution of crimes of assault and battery when perpetrated by male family members against women; even intrafamily murder and attempted murder rarely are prosecuted.[52] Consequently, much of this report deals almost exclusively with identifiable trends in the state response to non-familial sexual assault.

This report evaluates the different elements of the state's total failure to provide protection and effective remedies to women victims of violence. It takes a comprehensive look at the way the criminal justice system deals with cases of violence against women, focusing on the interaction between the police and legal establishments and the medicolegal system. Often overlooked, the maintenance of an efficient and responsive medicolegal system is a crucial part of the state's responsibility to ensure that survivors of assault have an effective remedy and that perpetrators of crimes are brought to justice. The current procedures for obtaining medical evidence in assault cases, particularly in cases of sexual assault of women, are woefully inadequate, neither ensuring that perpetrators are convicted nor

---

[50] Ibid.

[51] Human Rights Commission of Pakistan, *State of Human Rights in 1997*, p. 185.

[52] See generally Amnesty International, *Pakistan: Women's Human Rights Remain a Dead Letter*, (London: 1997).

providing women with appropriate treatment. Other barriers encountered by women victims of violence who attempt to navigate the criminal justice system include inveterate and widespread bias against them and their cases, official incompetence and corruption at all levels, systemic lack of professionalism and administrative inefficiency.

VI. THE STATE RESPONSE TO VIOLENCE AGAINST WOMEN

Domestic Law
Rape

In 1979 Pakistan's rape laws were dramatically changed when General Zia modified strategic aspects of the country's legal system in accordance with Islamic strictures. No longer part of the standard Penal Code, rape was included in the Offence of Zina Ordinance,[53] itself a subcategory of Zia's Enforcement of Hudood[54] Ordinance of 1979. The Zina Ordinance has had a profound effect on the rights of women, as it broadens the category of criminal sexual activity and redefines how such crimes will be handled by the legal system. The prohibited sexual activities, including rape (zina bil jabr), became religious offenses, subject to different standards of evidence and punishment and the appellate jurisdiction of Islamic higher courts.[55]

Pakistan's previous rape laws, repealed by the Zina Ordinance,[56] had defined rape as compulsory sexual intercourse. The new law added to this definition that both a man and a woman may be guilty of rape and narrowed the circumstances in which rape can be said to have occurred. Statutory rape, previously defined as sex with or without the consent of a girl under the age of 14, was no longer a crime.[57] In addition, the legal possibility of marital rape was eliminated; by definition, rape became an extra-marital offense.[58] The Zina

---

[53] Offence of Zina (Enforcement of Hudood) Ordinance, 1979 (hereinafter Zina Ordinance). The Zina Ordinance encompasses the crimes of zina, which can be translated as both adultery and fornication, and zina-bil-jabr, which can be translated as rape.

[54] The *Hudood* Ordinance is a set of Islamic penal laws introduced by General Zia ul-Haq in 1979 as part of his campaign to Islamicize the country's legal system. *Hudood* means "prevention, hindrance, restraint, prohibition and hence a restrictive ordinance or statute of Allah respecting things lawful and unlawful." See Lippman, McConville and Yerushalmi, *Islamic Criminal Law and Procedure: An Introduction* (New York: Praeger, 1988), p. 38.

[55] Only cases resulting in sentences of two years imprisonment or less may be appealed to the regular high courts.

[56] Sections 3 and 19(3), Offence of Zina (Enforcement of Hudood) Ordinance, 1979.

[57] See Pakistan Penal Code, Chapter XVI, Offenses Affecting the Human Body, of Rape, Section 375(5).

[58] Ironically, a woman can bring criminal proceedings against her husband for sodomy, a separate offense under Section 377 of the Pakistan Penal code, which also specifies other "unnatural offences."

Ordinance defined rape as sexual intercourse without being validly married whe it occurs in any of the following circumstances:

> (a) against the will of the victim; (b) without the consent of the victim; (c) with the consent of the victim, when the consent has been obtained by putting the victim in fear of death or of hurt; or (d) with the consent of the victim, when the offender knows that the offender is not validly married to the victim and that the consent is given because the victim believes that the offender is another person to whom the victim is or believes herself or himself to be validly married.[59]

A showing by the perpetrator that he was or believed he was validly married to th victim at the time of intercourse is a complete defense to the crime of zina-bil-jal or rape.[60]

Another significant change brought about by the adoption of the Zina law was that for the first time in Pakistan's history, fornication (non-marital se> became illegal and, along with adultery, non-compoundable,[61] non-bailable[62] an punishable at maximum by death. Since the crime of statutory rape was eliminate

---

[59] Section 6(1), Offence of Zina (Enforcement of Hudood) Ord., 1979.

[60] For example, in one 1997 case, a woman went to a Family Court to challeng the validity of her marriage, claiming that she had been abducted, forced to sig (thumbprint) a marriage certificate under threat of death, and then repeatedly raped by h(purported "husband." The defendant claimed that the woman had eloped with him and th; they had signed the marriage certificate in front of five witnesses; however, a Family Cour the civil court charged with ruling on the validity of the marriage, found the marriag certificate to be irregular. The defendant was charged with rape under subsection 10(2) (the Zina Ordinance and convicted by the trial court, but the Federal Shariat Court acquitte him on appeal. Disregarding the Family Court's ruling that the marriage was invalid an discrepancies in the accused's version of the facts, the appellate court held that "the willfi commission of zina cannot be alleged against a person who believes for good reasons th; the woman with whom he is having sexual intercourse was his wife and he had entered int marriage with her lawfully." 1997 P.Cr.L.J. 1666. Cited in Julie Dror Chadbourne, *Neve wear your shoes after midnight: Legal Trends Under the Pakistan Zina Ordinance*, pap(pending publication, on file with Human Rights Watch.

[61] A non-compoundable offense is one which the police or government ma continue to investigate and prosecute even if the original complainant withdraws his or h(statement implicating the accused.

[62] Those prosecuted on such charges are not eligible as of right for release pendin trial by posting bond. Bail is left to the discretion of the judge.

at the same time that fornication was criminalized, even minor girls can be charged with engaging in illicit sex if they have reached puberty.[63]

The punishment for illicit sex, be it adultery or rape, depends on both the evidence on which the conviction rests and the marital status of the offender. The maximum punishment is known as *Hadd* (literally, "the limit"), the singular of Hudood, and is a mandatory sentence that a judge may not mitigate. Hadd sentences are harsher for people who are married and Muslim *(muhsan)*:[64] if the accused is muhsan and (a) confesses or (b) there are four adult, pious, male Muslim witnesses to the act of penetration, then the accused must be sentenced to death by stoning.[65] If, on the other hand, the accused is non-muhsan and (a) confesses or (b) the crime is witnessed by four adult men, not necessarily Muslims, the accused must be sentenced to a hundred lashes with a whip.[66] The testimony of four female witnesses, let alone that of the victim alone, is not sufficient for the imposition of the Hadd punishment. A non-muhsan person convicted of rape may receive, in addition to a hundred lashes, "such other punishment, including the sentence of death, as the Court may deem fit having regard to the circumstances of the case."[67] All Hadd punishments must be confirmed by an appellate court.[68] To date, although Hadd punishments have been imposed, none has been carried out.

On account of their harshness, Hadd sentences require extraordinarily conclusive evidence. If the evidence falls short of the stringent (and discriminatory) threshold required for imposing the draconian Hadd punishments, the accused may be sentenced to a lesser class of punishment known as *Tazir*. It

---

[63] The Zina Ordinance applies to adults, defined as "a person who has attained, being a male, the age of eighteen years or, being a female, the age of sixteen years, or has attained puberty." Offence of Zina (Enforcement of Hudood) Ordinance, Section 2(a). For girls, menarche is sufficient to determine that puberty has been attained; thus, girls under the age of 16 who have begun menstruating may be liable for criminal prosecution under the Zina Ordinance.

[64] Offence of Zina (Enforcement of Hudood) Ord., 1979, Sections 5(2) and 6(3). Section 2 of the Ordinance defines the term *"Muhsan"* as "a Muslim adult man [woman] who is not insane and has had sexual intercourse with a Muslim adult woman [man] who, at the time he [she] had sexual intercourse with her [him], was married to him [her] and was not insane." In other words, a Muslim who has previously had sexual intercourse within a valid marriage faces stiffer sentences than a non-Muslim or a person who has not previously had licit sexual intercourse.

[65] Offence of Zina (Enforcement of Hudood) Ord., 1979, Section 8.

[66] Ibid.

[67] Ibid., Section 6(3)(b).

[68] Ibid., Sections 5(3) and 6(4).

is important to note that insufficient evidence to impose a Hadd punishment does not eliminate criminal liability: the Tazir punishment for rape is up to twenty-five years' imprisonment and thirty lashes. For the purposes of Tazir, no distinction is made between a muhsan and non-muhsan offender. Because of the strict evidentiary requirements for Hadd punishments, the overwhelming majority of rape cases are tried at the Tazir level of evidence and punishment.

Evidence for Tazir punishment is governed by the standard evidence code (*Qanun-e-Shahadat*) which was introduced by General Zia in 1984. The evidence code states:

> Unless otherwise provided in any law relating to the enforcement of Hudood ... in matters pertaining to financial or future obligations ... the instruments shall be attested to by two men or by one man and two women ... in all other matters, the court *may* accept, or act on, the testimony of one man or one woman.[69]

The use of the word "may" in the second part of the section provides for the admissibility of the testimony of women, but it does not guarantee that such testimony will be admitted or given equal weight to that of a man. At both the Hadd and Tazir levels of punishment, the burden of proof is on the prosecution to prove rape charges beyond a reasonable doubt.[70] There is a general rule that that the benefit of any doubt—as, for example, that created by contradictory testimony, unexplained gaps in testimony, or inconclusive expert testimony—be extended to the accused.

The only foolproof way to obtain a rape conviction is if the accused confesses[71] or there are four adult male witnesses to the act of penetration.[72]

---

[69] *Qanun-e-Shahadat Order*, 1984, Section 17 (emphasis added).

[70] *Mehboob Hussain*, PLD 1988 FSC 3.

[71] Confessions must be given four times in open court on separate occasions. This provision is designed to guard against coerced or false confessions. To satisfy the requirements of the law, a confession must be (a) unequivocal, (b) describe the criminal act in detail, and (c) must be corroborated by other evidence. See M. Mahmood, *Enforcement of Hudood, Practice and Procedure* (Lahore: Pakistan Law Times Publications, 1991), p. 574. A confession can be withdrawn at any time prior to the execution of sentence. In the case of a retracted confession, the finding of guilt may be nullified, but a conviction and lesser sentence may be meted out if there is independent corroborating evidence for the confession. See also *Najib Raza Rehmani v. The State*, PLD 1978 Supreme Court 200.

[72] Offence of Zina (Enforcement of Hudood) Ord., 1979, Section 8.

Otherwise, the courts have no consistent standards for proof of rape. For example, according to Section 6(1) of the Zina Ordinance, "Penetration is sufficient to constitute the sexual intercourse necessary to the offence of zina-bil-jabr,"[73] and the case law is clear that penetration must be by a penis and not other foreign objects;[74] however, the courts are divided over the extent of penetration required to constitute rape under the ordinance.[75] Similarly, there is no clarity in the case law as to the related question of what constitutes proof of penetration, although some corroborative evidence is required.[76] Some cases indicate that even the slightest penetration is sufficient;[77] numerous others discuss issues related to proof of penetration in terms of the presence of semen inside the vagina or a torn hymen, suggesting that evidence supporting full penetration is required.[78] Adding to the murkiness of the issue of proof of penetration, several cases have held that the presence of semen in the victim's vagina is an insufficient indication.[79]

Courts have also ruled inconsistently on what, if any, corroboration as to the non-consensual nature of the intercourse is required.[80] In general, courts are very reluctant to hand down rape convictions in cases where there are no "marks of violence" on the victim's body and the evidence consists solely of the victim's word against the defendant's.[81] Supporting physical evidence from the victim's body has been required to convict even in rape cases where consent has been

---

[73] Ibid.

[74] See 1996 P.Cr.L.J. 610 (penetration by a pen is insufficient for rape conviction), cited in Chadbourne, *Never wear your shoes.*

[75] Chadbourne, *Never wear your shoes.*

[76] Ibid.

[77] 1985 P.Cr.L.J. 110; PLJ 1985 FSC 20, cited in Chadbourne, *Never wear your shoes.*

[78] Ibid.

[79] 1993 P.Cr.L.J. 234 (PSC). Also see Chadbourne, *Never wear your shoes.*

[80] For example, one rape case (*Janoo*, PLJ 1982 FSC 68) has held that corroboration of a victim's testimony may not be necessary "unless the circumstances of the case indicate the possibility of consent," while another rape case (*Abid Hussain*, PLJ 1983 FSC 124) has held exactly the opposite: "Generally speaking corroboration is needed to support the version of the prosecutrix to convict the accused."

[81] 1996 P.Cr.L.J. 186, cited in Chadbourne, *Never wear your shoes.* In one 1996 rape case, the testimony of the rape victim alone was inadequate to secure a conviction. 1996 P.Cr.L.J. 612, cited in Chadbourne, *Never wear your Shoes.* However, in a 1997 appeals case, the court concluded that even without any marks of violence on the victim, the facts sugggest "that the case we are dealing with is a case of simple rape on a grown up adult female without brutality." 1997 P Cr.LJ 1114.

obtained through the threat of violence, for example at gunpoint, thus limiting the possibility of struggle.[82] On the basis of a presumption of female consent and a belief that women tend to lie in rape cases, judges ascribe undue significance to bodily evidence of the use of physical force by the defendant and physical, as opposed to verbal, resistance by the woman. For example, the Federal Shariat Court overturned a lower court's conviction of rape on the grounds that medical examiners "did not observe any injury on the thighs, legs, elbows, arms, knees, face, back and buttocks of the victim," and held that "she was bound to sustain injuries . . . as she was supposed to put up resistance."[83] Although some victims may have no chance of fending off an attacker, judges seem to require that they resist and also suffer visible physical injury if they wish to see their attackers punished.

In many rape cases where there is no supporting bodily evidence from the victim or defendant, courts have arbitrarily opted to convict the defendant of the lesser charge of adultery or fornication.[84] It appears that judges are reluctant, out of bias, to impose the significant penalties that attach to a conviction for rape but, in the face of the evidence, cannot let a defendant off entirely either. For example, a court in a 1997 rape case declared that in the absence of marks of violence on the victim's body and her failure on cross-examination to prove adequately that she resisted the defendant's advances, "[the] offence of zina-bil-jabr, thus having not been made out against the accused his conviction under S. 10(3) [the section of the Zina Ordinance establishing the crime of zina-bil-jabr or rape] was altered to S. 10(2) [the section of the Ordinance codifying the crime of zina or adultery/fornication]."[85] Similarly, the Federal Shariat Court converted a rape conviction to one of fornication on the grounds that "[s]ince no violence was found on her body, it could be reasonable to infer that she was a willing party to sexual intercourse."[86] These cases demonstrate that, based on prejudiced evidentiary requirements and interpretation stemming from a disinclination to credit female testimony about rape, courts at times spontaneously and unilaterally alter the nature of the charges leveled by the prosecution and convict the defendant of the lesser

---

[82]Ubaidullah v. The State, PLD 1983 FSC 117, cited in Chadbourne, *Never wear your shoes*.

[83] PLD 1987 FSC 11.

[84] NLR 1987 SD 1985, cited in Chadbourne, *Never wear your shoes*.

[85] *Mohammad Ikram alias Munji v. The State*, 1997 P.Cr.L.J. 1079, cited in Chadbourne, *Never wear your shoes*.

[86] *Ubaidullah v. The State*, PLD 1983 FSC 117, cited in Chadbourne, *Never Wear Your Shoes*.

crime of illegal consensual sex instead of rape. In such instances, a corresponding prosecution is not necessarily initiated against the complainant, but the potential for it is created.[87]

An even worse scenario resulting from judges' reluctance to convict in rape cases is that courts sometimes view a woman's charge of rape as an admission of illegal sex unless she can prove, by their standards, that the intercourse was non-consensual and therefore not fornication or adultery. Thus the structure of the Zina Ordinance, and its interpretation by courts, leaves rape victims constantly susceptible to prosecution for illicit consensual sex. As Dr. Justice Javid Iqbal has written, "[T]he court considers the aggrieved party or prosecutrix guilty until she proves herself innocent...Thus, when a woman files such a complaint [of rape], instead of seeking justice she places herself at the mercy of the court."[88]

In the early years of the Zina ordinance especially, it was not uncommon for the female victim in rape cases to be prosecuted for adultery or fornication unless she provided extraordinarily conclusive proof that her "participation" in impermissible intercourse was forced;[89] the accused rapist, on the other hand, was usually acquitted of all charges.[90] Such cases revealed that the standard of proof beyond a reasonable doubt was not applied equally, or, put another way, the benefit of the doubt that was rightfully accorded to men accused of rape was often not equally extended to women whose rape charges had been converted into charges against them of illegal consensual sex. While the courts generally required rape charges to be proven beyond a reasonable doubt, they would often accept a

---

[87] See, generally, Chadbourne, *Never Wear Your Shoes*.

[88] Dr. Justice Javid Iqbal, translated by Professor Nasira Iqbal, "Crimes Against Women in Pakistan," *Journal of South Asian and Middle Eastern Studies,* vol. 13, no. 3, pp. 37-48.

[89] Under Pakistan's Evidence Code whether a woman sought immediate assistance following her rape can be factor in determining whether her complaint is true. In the United States, this requirement is known as the "fresh complaint rule," which, according to *Black's Law Dictionary*, Fifth Edition (1979), provides that in sexual assault cases, proof that the alleged victim did not complain of the assault within a "reasonable" time after it occurred, to a person to whom she would ordinarily turn for help, is admissible to denigrate the credibility of the victim. This rule has been widely discredited in the United States and Europe because it has been used to create the presumption that women who fail to report rapes may not have in fact been raped. The rule fails to acknowledge the many sound reasons why women might fail to report rape including, in the context of Pakistan, the risk of criminal prosecution if they fail to prove their case.

[90] See Human Rights Watch, *Double Jeopardy: Police Abuse of Women in Pakistan*, (New York: Human Rights Watch, 1992), pp. 53-60.

woman's rape allegation—once disproved—as *prima facie* evidence that she engaged in consensual extramarital sex, despite the fact that a failure to demonstrate rape (coerced sex) beyond a reasonable doubt does not automatically prove beyond a reasonable doubt that consensual sex occurred. Such cases are far less frequent in the late 1990s than they were in the 1980s, and some courts have explicitly ruled that a woman's failure to prove an allegation of rape does not constitute *prima facie* evidence of her participation in illicit consensual sex.[91]

Despite these few positive developments and trends, the continued enforcement of the discriminatory Zina Ordinance, inconsistent rulings by the courts, and gender bias in the criminal justice system makes it extraordinarily difficult for rape victims to get justice and continues to leave them vulnerable to wrongful prosecution for adultery or fornication.

Domestic Violence

Pakistani law is even more inadequate in protecting women victims of domestic violence and penalizing batterers. Not explicitly prohibited by a specific, targeted, and distinct set of laws, most acts of domestic violence are encompassed by the Qisas and Diyat Ordinance of 1990,[92] a body of Islamic criminal laws dealing with murder, attempted murder, and the crime of causing bodily "hurt"[93]

---

[91] See, e.g., *Mst. Rani v. The State*, PLD 1996 Karachi 316.

[92] The Criminal Law (Second Amendment) Ordinance, 1990, commonly known as the Qisas and Diyat Ordinance, 1990, amended the Pakistan Penal Code (Sections 299 to 338) and the Code of Criminal Procedure. The Qisas and Diyat Ordinance, which had been kept in force by invoking the president's power to re-issue it every four months, was formally enacted into law in April 1997. Under Article 89 of the Constitution, the president is empowered to promulgate an ordinance if the the National Assembly is not in session and circumstances require immediate legislation. An ordinance lapses in four months if it is not endorsed sooner by the assembly. The Human Rights Commission of Paksitan (HRCP) has severely criticized the use of ordinances by several presidents to bypass parliamentary debate and govern without national consensus, as well as the practice of reintroducing, time and again, the same ordinance when the specified four-month period has lapsed without action by the National Assembly. In it annual report for 1997,
HRCP also criticized the manner in which the Qisas and Diyat Ordinance of 1990 was finally enacted into law in 1997: "The relevant bill was rushed through parliament without debate and the president gave his assent forthwith. The opposition's plea that this important and controversial measure needed fullest possible discussion was ignored." Human Rights Commission of Pakistan, *State of Human Rights in 1997*, p. 34.

[93] Section 332 of the Pakistan Penal Code defines "hurt" as follows: "Whoever causes pain, harm, disease, infirmity or injury to any person or impairs, disables or dismembers any organ of the body or part thereof [of] any person without causing his death,

The State Response to Violence Against Women

(both intentional and unintentional). In the absence of explicit criminalization of domestic violence, police and judges have tended to treat it as a non-justiciable, private or family matter or, at best, an issue for civil, rather than criminal, courts.[94]

If a domestic violence case does come before a criminal court, it may be punished either by qisas (retribution) or diyat (compensation) for the benefit of the victim or his or her legal heirs. In qisas and diyat crimes, the victim or heir has the right to determine whether to exact retribution or compensation or to pardon the accused.[95] If the victim or heir chooses to waive qisas, or qisas is judicially held to be inapplicable, an offender is subject to tazir or discretionary punishment in the form of imprisonment.[96] In these instances, judges not only have the power to determine the extent of punishment but also to decide whether to punish the offender at all.[97]

Commentators have noted that the qisas and diyat laws have, in many respects, converted serious crimes, including murder and aggravated assault, into crimes against the individual rather than the state. One Pakistani researcher has written, "By vesting the primary right of forgiveness in the individual for such a serious crime as murder, the state has exposed the most susceptible sections of society to pressure from the powerful."[98]

---

is said to cause hurt."

[94] See Yasmine Hassan, *The Haven Becomes Hell*, (Lahore: Shirkat Gah, 1995), pp. 57, 60.

[95] Where an injury has been inflicted, the offender is liable to an identical injury or equal amount of hurt as qisas punishment. Qisas is to be executed in public by a medical practitioner. Owing to the focus on exact retribution, qisas and diyat crimes are categorized according to, among others factors, the nature and extent of the injury caused. Hence, medicolegal doctors, who assess and document the injury, play a role in the framing of charges.

[96] The Federal Shariat Court (an Islamic appellate court) has indicated that only crimes against the rights of God should be subject to tazir, not crimes against the rights of man. Distinguishing between the two categories of crimes involves determining whether the offender poses a threat to society at large. See Evan Gottesman, "The Reemergence of Qisas and Diyat in Pakistan," *Columbia Human Rights Law Review*, v. 23, n. 2, pp. 433-461.

[97] If the victim or heir waives qisas, the state has reserved the right unilaterally to imprison an offender for up to ten years where warranted by the "facts and circumstances of the case,"and to impose sentences of up to fourteen years in prison for repeat offenders. Pakistan Penal Code, Section 311.

[98] *Trend of Superior Courts*, unpublished paper, p. 10, on file with Human Rights Watch.

The "privatization" of crimes by the qisas and diyat laws has particularly damaging consequences in cases of intrafamily violence, the majority of which involve domestic abuse or spousal murder. As a result of the law, not only are women victims of domestic violence and their heirs susceptible to pressure and intimidation to waive qisas, but the concept of monetary compensation can be meaningless in a situation where payments flow from one member of the nuclear family to another.[99]

Furthermore, murder (*Qatl-e-Amd*) is not liable to qisas "when any *wali* [heir] of the victim is a direct descendant, how low-so-ever, of the offender."[100] Thus, cases in which a woman has been murdered by her husband would be exempt from the qisas or maximum (i.e., capital) punishment for the murder if the couple in question have children, since in that case, a child or heir of the victim would also be a direct descendant of the offender.[101] Diyat in such cases, entailing compensation flowing from a father to his (motherless) children, would be a mockery. Although courts can impose tazir punishment in a spousal murder case of this kind, the maximum they can award is fourteen years' imprisonment. Moreover, courts are directed to weigh the decision to impose tazir punishment "having regard to the facts and circumstances of the case," which grants them a large measure of discretion.[102] In light of the biased attitudes of the courts with respect to domestic violence, the fact that punishment in such cases of spousal murder has been left entirely to the discretion of judges may well spell total impunity for the most extreme form of domestic violence. In the words of one commentator, "Although it is still unclear how the law will be applied in practice, it may be a means by which the state abdicates its responsibility to control violence in the most common type of intrafamily murder—the killing of a female member by the male head of the family."[103]

The large degree of judical discretion embodied in the qisas and diyat law has been widely criticized in light of the endemic societal and judical discrimination against women in Pakistan. Among the dangers that arise from

---

[99] Miranda Davies, ed., *Women and Violence*, (Atlantic Highlands, N.J.: Zed Books, 1994), p. 217.

[100] Pakistan Penal Code, Section 306(c).

[101] Human Rights Watch opposes the infliction of capital punishment in all circumstances because of its inherent cruelty.

[102] Pakistan Penal Code, Section 308(2).

[103] Davies, *Women and Violence*, p. 217.

decodification and an increase in judicial discretion is the opportunity for discrimination and corruption.[104]

When the qisas and diyat laws were first proposed in the early 1980s during General Zia's Islamization campaign, the testimony of women was not accepted in the execution of qisas, which meant that a woman accused of committing an offense requiring retribution was not allowed to testify on her own behalf. Moreover, when the victim was a woman, the amount of diyat was halved.[105] The language of the current law does not distinguish between the sexes with regard to payment of diyat, but both the amount of the diyat and the validity of a woman's testimony have been left to judicial discretion, the former to be decided "subject to the Injunctions of Islam as laid down in the Holy Qur'an and Sunnah."[106] Since traditional interpretations of Islamic law contemplate the diyat for a woman victim to be half of that for a man, the gender neutral language of the current codified law on diyat is practically meaningless. And the invitation to exercise discretion with regard to the testimony of women in effect encourages judges to manifest their own prejudices and biases against women. The law of inheritance, which governs the distribution of diyat among heirs, is also discriminatory to women, as the shares of female heirs are typically smaller than those of their male counterparts. In addition, the Human Rights Commission of Pakistan noted, "[H]eirs entitled to . . . diyat, were mostly assumed by the law to be male. It was observed that where the blood money [diyat] had to go to a female, the courts, which were responsible for fixing the amount, tended to be less liberal."[107]

Honor killings are another form of intrafamily violence with victims who are mostly women, who are seen as the repositories of family honor.[108] Such killings are also encompassed by the murder provisions of the qisas and diyat laws. However, courts minimize the severity of these crimes by applying to them, in effect, the English common law principle of "grave and sudden provocation."[109]

---

[104] Evan Gottesman, "The Reemergence of Qisas and Diyat in Pakistan," *Columbia Human Rights Law Review*, v.23, n.2, pp. 434-5.

[105] Asma Jahangir, "A Pound of Flesh," *Newsline* (Karachi), December 1990, pp. 61-62.

[106] Pakistan Penal Code Sections 323 and 304(b). See also Qanun-e-Shahadat Order, 1984, section 17, and Jahangir, "A Pound of Flesh," pp. 61-62.

[107] Human Rights Commission of Pakistan, *State of Human Rights in 1997*, p. 182.

[108] Ibid., p. 187.

[109] This principle was traditionally used to reduce charges of murder to those of manslaughter in cases where the accused was deemed to have acted on the basis of a provocation that caused him to temporily lose self-control. The law recognized only certain

In so doing, courts simply deem that qisas is not applicable to honor killings, and punish these crimes under Section 302(c) of the Pakistan Penal Code (as amended by the qisas and diyat ordinance), which allows for punishment of murder with imprisonment up to twenty-five years where qisas is not applicable. In practice, however, punishments meted out under this section tend to be lenient in such cases.

For example, the Human Rights Commission of Pakistan reported a case in which a man was tried for killing his daughter and a young man when he found them in a "compromising state." The sessions (trial court) judge sentenced the father to life imprisonment and a fine of Rs. 20,000 (U.S.$ 500). The case came before the Lahore High Court, which reduced the sentence to five years' imprisonment and a fine of Rs. 10,000 ($250).[110] In its judgment drastically reducing the defendant's sentence, the appellate court indicated that his actions were justified because his victims were engaging in immoral behavior that could not be tolerated in an Islamic state such as Pakistan.[111]

Courts have used other means as well to remove honor killings cases from the ambit of qisas punishment and bring them within Section 302(c) of the amended Pakistan Penal Code (P.P.C.), which permits judges to impose discretionary punishment "where according to the Injunctions of Islam the punishment of qisas is not applicable." For example, in a case where a husband killed a man upon finding him with his wife at night in a "compromising" position, the court ruled that "*Qatl-e-Amd* [murder] liable to qisas takes place only when the person murdered is not liable to be murdered and is *masoom-ud-dam* [innocent]. Apparently the offence of the appellant attracts section 302(c) P.P.C. [because as an adulterer the victim was not innocent] where under imprisonment could be up to twenty-five years, because qisas is not applicable."[112] Another court using discretionary authority granted by Section 338-F of the amended P.P.C., which "expressly permits the court to assess the culpability of . . . the accused not only under the statutory provisions of law but also under the injunctions of Qur'an and Sunnah," decided that "the right of self-defence is wider under Islamic law than in the [amended] P.P.C." and could be invoked by male defendants in honor killings.[113] The court explained that the Koranic verse 34 of *Sura Al-Nisa*

---

provocations in this regard, including coming upon one's wife in the act of being unfaithful. Women who killed their husbands for the same reason were generally not granted a similar mitigation of charges.

[110] Human Rights Commission of Pakistan, *State of Human Rights in 1997*, p. 76.
[111] Ibid.
[112] *Trend of Superior Courts*, unpublished paper, p. 17.
[113] Ibid.

establishes men as the "custodians of women;" hence a man who kills another man for defiling the honor of his wife or daughter is protecting his property and acting in self-defense. Quoting *Sura Al-Nisa*, the judge concluded, "I am of the view that the appellant as the custodian of the honor of his wife had the right to kill the deceased while he was engaged in [a] sex act with his wife and he had not earned liability of qisas or tazir or even diyat, and is hereby acquitted."[114]

Ironically, "self-defense" and "grave and sudden provocation" were specified as exceptions to murder in the unamended P.P.C. and were removed from the books when the qisas and diyat laws were incorporated into the code. However, by coupling a significant increase in courts' discretionary powers with instructions to rely on the "Injunctions of Islam,"[115] the qisas and diyat laws have actually broadened the scope of these exceptions. This is but one indication of the greater leeway granted judges by this new legislation to exercise their prejudices in the name of law.[116]

Gender Bias in the Criminal Justice System

Through interviews with human rights lawyers and activists, women victims of violence, police officials, prosecutors, judges, and medicolegal doctors, Human Rights Watch found that bias against female victims of rape and domestic violence is not confined to the letter and interpretation of the law. Rather, it pervades all facets of the Pakistani criminal justice system. From the initial lodging of complaints until the final resolution of cases, women seeking redress for sexual and other assault regularly confront law enforcement institutions and officials with hostile, or at best indifferent, attitudes to their complaints. Police, prosecutors, judges, and doctors denied that sexual and domestic violence were critical problems for women and asserted that the occurrence of such crimes was precluded by Pakistani social and religious norms. Officials even failed consistently to acknowledge the criminal status of domestic violence, instead dismissing it as a "family matter" not serious enough to be handled by the criminal justice system. Officials frequently justified their cynical attitude toward women's complaints of sexual and other assaults by attacking their veracity. Rather than addressing any inadequacies of the system with respect to prosecuting rape or domestic violence, officials were more interested in pointing out how frequently women fabricate these charges in order to frame men.

---

[114] Ibid.
[115] See, e.g., Section 338F of the Pakistan Penal Code.
[116] *Trend of Superior Courts*, unpublished paper, p. 14.

Skepticism and scorn about women's complaints of violence are rife among police officials, who function as gatekeepers with respect to women's access to the criminal justice system. For example, Ashiq Martha, the chief or Station House Officer (SHO) of Ichra Thana, a busy Lahore police station, told Human Rights Watch that non-consensual sexual intercourse virtually does not exist in Pakistan and that in the overwhelming majority of cases women fabricate allegations of rape. According to SHO Martha, rape only occurs in two situations: if the man is of unsound mind or if he acts to avenge his honor against the woman's family. He added that the absence of visible marks of violence would prove that intercourse was consensual.[117] In a similar vein, the SHO of the Factory Road police station in Lahore told Human Rights Watch that genuine rape cases, along with kidnappings and abductions of women, are extremely rare and that in most instances women run off with men willingly and then lie to avoid being prosecuted for adultery. He added that complainants disingenuously press charges of attempted rape over minor disputes or fabricate charges of sexual violence to settle personal scores. He believed that "[w]omen have a lot of rights" and that "[i]t is wrong of courts to believe women so that the poor man ends up in jail." The SHO of the Women's Police Station[118] in Karachi, Farrukh Sultana, asserted, "Rape is indicated by marks of violence on the woman. In consensual cases there are no

---

[117] Human Rights Watch interview, SHO Ashiq Martha, Ichra Thana police station, Lahore, April 14, 1997.

[118] Karachi and Lahore each have a Women's Police Station. "Special women's police stations were established in 1994 in response to growing numbers of complaints of custodial abuse of women, including rape. These police stations are staffed by female personnel, but receive even less material and human resources than regular police stations, according to human rights advocates. According to the Government's own Commission of Inquiry for Women, the stations do not function independently or fulfill their purpose. Despite court orders and regulations requiring that female suspects be interrogated only by female police officers, women continued to be detained overnight at regular police stations and abused by male officers. In a study of Lahore newspapers from January to July 1997, the Commission of Inquiry for Women found 52 cases of violence or torture of women while in police custody. A woman, 'Nasreen,' accused the SHO of Lahore's Mozang police station of raping her on August 25, after she visited the station to register a complaint against her in-laws. The case is under internal investigation by Lahore police." U.S. Department of State, *Pakistan Country Report on Human Rights Practices for 1998* (Washington: U.S. Department of State, 1999), p.5. Although the initiative to establish women's police stations is well-intentioned, women's rights advocates argue that many more such stations are needed, with expanded powers and better trained staff, before they can have a positive impact.

marks, though the woman calls it rape anyway."[119] An NGO activist working with rape victims in Karachi told Human Rights Watch that an officer at the Women's Police Station had once said to her that rape only occurs with very young girls. Echoing the sentiments and proclivities of her colleagues, a senior police officer at the women's police station in Lahore told Human Rights Watch, "One can tell from looking at the woman if it is a [genuine] rape case. If there are no marks of violence and no circumstantial evidence, the woman can have lied about rape."[120] The comments of police officials to Human Rights Watch consistently indicated a simplistic and biased understanding of the dynamics of rape, a lack of knowledge and imagination as to the range of circumstances in which rapes of women occur, and a predisposition to disbelieve victims of rape.

Police officials in Karachi and Lahore also dismissed domestic violence as a non-issue. The director of the police training center in Lahore, for example, told Human Rights Watch, "The social set-up [in Pakistan] does not allow that women should be abused" and that, on the contrary, women are respected in Pakistani society. When asked about the form of domestic abuse commonly referred to as "wife burning" or "dowry death" in Pakistan, the director responded that women burned to death because "stoves were defective" and that "if someone wants to kill there are other means."[121] Not a single police official interviewed by Human Rights Watch in either city acknowledged the seriousness of crimes of violence against women or expressed concern over their widespread and unchecked incidence.

Even the medicolegal doctors who are responsible for collecting forensic medical evidence to verify a woman's allegation of assault are unlikely to believe the complainants. The head medicolegal officer for Karachi, Dr. Nizamuddin Memon, who oversees all medicolegal services in the area, revealed to Human Rights Watch a strong bias against the plight of women victims.[122] He almost categorically denied the existence of rape, saying, "A woman who is well developed cannot be raped unless there are four or five men [involved]. One man cannot rape a woman. Only children under five are raped . . . [otherwise] rape is only gang rape. One-on-one cannot be rape unless a gun or other arms are used."

---

[119] Human Rights Watch interview, Farrukh Sultana, Karachi, May 12, 1997.

[120] Human Rights Watch interview, Women's Police Station, Lahore, May 3, 1997.

[121] Human Rights Watch interview, S.M. Shafiq, Director of Research at Punjab Police Special Branch Headquarters, Women's Police Station, Lahore, November 6, 1996.

[122] Human Rights Watch interview, Dr. Nizamuddin Memon, Office of the Police Surgeon, Karachi, April 22, 1997.

He asserted that women lie when they allege that they were raped by an unassisted man and that he had exposed women brought to the police surgeon's office[123] to be liars by closely questioning them: "Women bluff, women make up stories, women lie. They say, 'I was drugged, I was given a whiff of fainting medicine'—but there's no such medicine. Even if a chicken is abducted it makes a noise. How can a woman be abducted? It's the boy who suffers in these cases because he gets to spend fourteen years in jail on the basis of false allegations of rape." Dr. Memon told Human Rights Watch about an examinee who came to his office alleging that her brother had repeatedly raped her: "The police had believed her, but I did not. Fathers may rape daughters, often in old age when they are mentally off, but brothers do not go that far." He further asserted that there was no question of rape in the absence of visible marks of violence on the purported victim's body.[124]

A member of a legal aid organization for women told us about an incident in 1996 when she took two minor girls, recently released from a brothel, to the Karachi police surgeon's office for medicolegal examinations. When she informed the police surgeon that the girls were victims of sexual abuse and not prostitutes as he had assumed, he replied, "For you, everyone is a victim. These girls were willing participants."[125] He declared that a ten-year-old was capable of consent in this context. A male medicolegal officer at the police surgeon's office, Karachi, told Human Rights Watch, "All girls who come here for an examination have gone [to have sex] willingly, and the poor boy gets stuck in jail for his whole life. Usually the girl's parents force her to change her story and testify falsely against the boy."[126] Dr. Sikander Shah, then chief chemical examiner[127] for Karachi, expressed similar sentiments to Human Rights Watch. Asked about rape cases, he said, "Most women go with men willingly, then change their story under pressure . . . God has protected justice by giving women hymens. Hymens cannot be repaired. So we know if she complains of rape whether she's lying."[128] Again, the only concern voiced by Dr. Abbas, who oversees the section of the chemical examiner's office (government forensic laboratory) in Lahore that analyzes

---

[123] The Police Surgeon for Karachi is the chief of medicolegal services for the metropolitan area.

[124] Ibid.

[125] Human Rights Watch interview, Karachi, May 16, 1997.

[126] Human Rights Watch interview, Office of Police Surgeon, Karachi, April 22, 1997.

[127] The chemical examiner's office analyzes the forensic evidence collected by the medicolegal doctors.

[128] Human Rights Watch interview, Dr. Sikander Shah, Karachi, November, 1996.

semen,[129] was that better forensic techniques were required to protect men from false accusations of rape; he made no reference to the dire need for improved forensic work in order to convict perpetrators of violence against women. He complained that the laboratory currently only tested for the presence of semen in a woman's vaginal sample, which could serve to incriminate men but did not afford them the means to exonerate themselves: "At least semen grouping[130] should be regularly done, and best of all [the availability of] a DNA test would help out an innocent fellow."[131] Ironically, simple semen detection does not particularly help a woman's case either, since it reveals no identifying information; semen grouping and DNA testing would far more accurately connect perpetrators to their crimes.

Victims of domestic violence rarely even make it to the medicolegal office, because few cases of domestic violence are prosecuted. Those women who are persistent enough to press criminal charges face similar skepticism from medicolegal doctors. When asked whether victims of domestic violence were examined at his office, Captain Memon replied, "Twenty-five percent of such women come with self-inflicted wounds. This is on their lawyers' advice so that they can get a divorce. Otherwise it is difficult to get a divorce." He added that women alleging rape also "self-inflict marks."[132]

Biased and chauvinistic attitudes are also common among prosecutors. An activist with a Karachi NGO that provides legal assistance to rape victims told Human Rights Watch that when she tried to give the organization's newsletter to a prosecutor, he scoffed and asked her why she was bothering with women who were no better than prostitutes.[133] Revealing unabashed and categorical gender bias, a prosecutor from the Lahore District Attorney's office told Human Rights Watch that he had heard of a conviction in one rape case, but he felt that the woman and her family had fabricated the charge since the defendant had repeatedly alleged his innocence. He further explained, "I don't believe in rape cases. Women's consent is always there. If rape exists, it happens in only 1 percent of cases. For example, women may be raped during a *dacoity* [ambush by armed men], but that is an extremely rare case. Our society does not allow rape."[134] A

---

[129] Referred to in this report as the "semen section."
[130] Similar to blood grouping or typing, semen grouping would exclude men of a different semen group.
[131] Human Rights Watch interview, Dr. Abbas, Lahore, May 2, 1997.
[132] Ibid.
[133] Human Rights Watch interview, Karachi, May 16, 1997.
[134] Human Rights Watch interview, District and Sessions Court prosecutor, Lahore, May 3, 1997.

lower-level prosecutor, Police Inspector Legal Naseer Ahmed of the Model Town Courts, Lahore, told Human Rights Watch that virtually all rape cases are fabricated. "After all," he said, "if a man tries to rape a woman, she can slap him."[135] Even the advocate general of Punjab,[136] Khalid Ranjha, denied that rape is a problem in Pakistan. In fact, when told about SHO Ashiq Martha's comments, he replied, "The SHO is right. In Pakistan there is no rape as a consequence of sexual frustration. Rape may only occur in the context of honor [feuds]. Rape in the west is a sickness. Ours is not a sick society."[137] Assistant Public Prosecutor, District West, Karachi, Islamuddin Ayubi verbalized a common notion in Pakistan in his comment, "Rape is an issue with unmarried women. With married women, generally there is consent."[138] When asked about domestic violence, Ayubi responded, "But that is a family matter. It is handled by the family courts."[139] Although he admitted, upon prompting, that it can constitute criminal assault, he appeared bewildered and said that he had never heard of any criminal case of domestic violence brought before the courts.

Even judges, rather than dispensing justice, frequently give free rein to biases against women in the name of the law and harass women victims of violence. Zia Awan, a prominent human rights lawyer in Karachi, told Human Rights Watch about a domestic violence incident that he reported to a judge presiding over a related dispute between the couple in question.[140] The judge dismissed the complaint and directed a dumbfounded Awan to a verse of the Koran, *Sura Nur*, which he interpreted as permitting a husband to beat his wife. Another human rights activist working with rape victims told Human Rights Watch about the harassment meted out to the complainant in a rape case by the presiding judge in the Malir district court, Karachi. As the defense counsel cross-examined the complainant over her claim that she had been abducted by the defendant and forced at gunpoint to take a train, the judge scornfully interjected that even a goat would have struggled under the circumstances and that it was unbelievable that the complainant had taken no action and not even activated the train's emergency brake. Later, the same judge yelled at the complainant, who got irritated at being repeatedly asked the same question, to show respect to the defense counsel. He

---

[135] Human Rights Watch interview, Police Inspector Legal Naseer Ahmed, Lahore, May 3, 1997.
[136] The advocate general is the chief attorney for the government of Punjab.
[137] Human Rights Watch interview, Khalid Ranjha, Lahore, April 30, 1997.
[138] Human Rights Watch interview, Islamuddin Ayubi, Karachi, May 15, 1997.
[139] Ibid.
[140] Human Rights Watch interview, Zia Awan, Karachi, April 23, 1997.

threatened that if she was not deferential he would lock her up for adultery. He added, with reference to the complainant, "These women take off knowingly and willingly and then show up in court to make our lives difficult."[141] Even Judge Javed Qaisar, who is generally regarded as upstanding and sympathetic by women's rights advocates, told Human Rights Watch, "Generally speaking, there can be no sex without the woman's consent—I am telling you this as a man. If the woman is drugged or intoxicated, or is a minor, she can be raped. However, a man cannot be potent if he is worried that he will be caught in the act. To rape, a man has to prepare a lot. He cannot just go do it unless he is 'high' or in an altered mental state. In that state, though, he is still legally 100 percent liable."[142]

Courts have also demonstrated strong gender bias in their approach to incest cases, at times utterly rejecting the possibility of its occurrence.[143] A prosecutor from the Lahore district attorney's office told Human Rights Watch, "Incest does not occur here, though people might attempt it with small children between the ages of six and twelve."[144] In a 1988 case,[145] the Federal Shariat Court acquitted a man convicted and sentenced to the maximum punishment in two different trials for raping his nine-year-old daughter "[i]n essence . . . because [the court] could not accept that a father would rape or even abuse his own flesh and blood. Similarly, the Supreme Court of Pakistan stated in *Liaquat Ali* that the issue of whether a father *can* commit zina-bil-jabr with his *real* daughter 'need[ed] serious probe.'"[146]

Societal misperceptions and the reluctance by law enforcement officials to investigate violence against women has created an environment in Pakistan

---

[141] Human Rights Watch interview, human rights activist (name withheld upon request), Karachi, May 7, 1997.

[142] Human Rights Watch interview, Additional Sessions Judge Javed Qaiser, District West, Karachi, Karachi, May 15, 1997.

[143] Some judges, however, have not hesitated to hand down convictions in incest cases. In one case, the court went even further and ruled that a young girl could not, by definiton, consent to sexual intercourse with her father, because "even if no threat was given, the very position of command, supervision, sustenance, shelter and protection which [a] father possesse[s] as against his daughter constitute[s] sufficient compulsion that resistance or abstinence cannot be expected." 1997 P.Cr.L.J. 1351, *Muhammad Ashraf v. The State*, cited in Chadbourne, *Never wear your shoes*.

[144] Human Rights Watch interview, District and Sessions Court prosecutor, Lahore, May 3, 1997.

[145] Crim. Appeal No. 288/L of 1988, *Masood Aziz*, cited in Julie Dror Chadbourne, *Never wear your shoes*.

[146] Chadbourne, *Never wear your shoes* (emphasis in original).

where this violence, despite its prevalence, is rarely acknowledged and punished as a crime. Although there have been cases of women alleging rape in order to avoid adultery charges, law enforcement officials generally approach cases of sexual and other violence against women with an unwarranted degree of skepticism and unacceptable level of prejudice. Until government officials are made to apply even-handed laws that explicitly reject common prejudices and gender stereotypes, perpetrators of violence against women will remain unpunished, and the violence will continue unabated.

Role of the Police

Upon receiving a report of rape, assault, or domestic violence, the police should immediately register a First Information Report (FIR) detailing the nature of the crime;[147] contact a magistrate's office, which should be available twenty-four hours a day, to request a medicolegal exam; and then escort the complainant to the medicolegal office for an exam. The police are also responsible for investigating the incident[148] and delivering the results of the medicolegal exam and any other evidence to the prosecutor to bolster his or her case against the defendant. None of the women Human Rights Watch interviewed in Karachi or Lahore had their cases handled in this way.

Delayed and Mishandled Processing of Complaints

In practice, women who try to report rape, sexual assault, or domestic violence encounter a police system that is, at best, incompetent and sometimes outright abusive. Since the police system is generally the point of first contact with the criminal justice system, women victims, in seeking justice for sexual or other

---

[147] Criminal Procedure Code, 1898, sections 154, 155; Police Rules, 1934, Chapter XXIV, Rule 24-1.

[148] Pakistan's Criminal Procedure Code distinguishes between "cognizable" and "non-cognizable" offenses. A cognizable offense is one for "which a police officer, may, . . . arrest without warrant." A non-cognizable offence is one for "which a police officer may not arrest without warrant" (Sections 4 (f) and (n)). In cognizable cases, once an officer has registered an FIR, he or she may investigate the charge but there is no requirement to do so nor does it appear that there are any guidelines for making such a decision (Criminal Procedure Code, section 156; Police Rules, Chapter XXV, Rule 25-1). In non-cognizable cases, a police officer may not initiate an investigation without first securing an order from a judicial magistrate (Criminal Procedure Code, section 155(2)). Cases arising under the Hudood Ordinances, including rape, are cognizable, as the Ordinances provide for arrest without warrant.

The State Response to Violence Against Women 53

assault, encounter obstacles from the very beginning of the process. Virtually all the human rights lawyers and activists we interviewed reported that harassment, intimidation, physical abuse, and bribery of persons seeking the services of the police were common phenomena, indicating endemic corruption and a serious lack of accountability and professionalism in the police force. Women who allege rape or abuse and their families are particularly vulnerable to police misconduct owing to women's low status in Pakistani society, the stigma that is still attached to rape and domestic abuse, and the gender bias common among police. As a result of the latter, the police are prone to disbelieve and belittle women victims, particularly when they allege rape or domestic violence.

Summary rejection of their complaints without investigation is the most common problem encountered by women victims of violence at the police station. In fact, the reputation of the police is so uniformly bad in this respect that many women are deterred from reporting violence and consider contacting the police to be a futile endeavor. For many victims, the experience of confronting skeptical, dismissive, and venal police officers serves to intensify the trauma of the assault itself. Experienced NGO activists who provide legal assistance to women victims of violence told Human Rights Watch that they aim to bypass the police and take their clients directly before a magistrate to obtain an order instructing the police to register a complaint. However, this procedure is only possible through the intervention of legal aid workers with ongoing relationships with magistrates and is not normally available to abused women.

According to Pakistani human rights activists and advocates, there are several reasons behind the stonewalling of complaints by the police besides the tendency to disbelieve women alleging violence. The unchecked corruption that permeates the police force nationwide is a primary factor.[149] The police commonly stall on registering complaints in order to create leverage to demand bribes from both the complainant and the accused in blatant moves to obstruct justice.[150] We also found cases in which the police intimidated or pressured complainants to drop charges after accepting bribes from the accused. Many times police officers do not register FIRs simply because doing so would indicate a crime increase that would

---

[149] See Shazreh Hussein, with the Simorgh Collective, *Rape* (Lahore: Simorgh Collective, 1990), p.67. Although this study was published in 1990, human rights activists in Pakistan confirmed that its findings about police corruption were still relevant in the late 1990s.

[150] "[T]he reasons for this dereliction of duty is [sic] due to rampant corruption of the police force; the degree of extortion will depend on the financial position of the persons involved." Ibid.

not be well received by their superiors.[151] Finally, owing to sexist attitudes and a lack of training with respect to the scope of the law, the police are often reluctant to tackle sexual and domestic violence as full-fledged crimes. Instead, they tend to see their role in such cases as that of a mediator and frequently block or delay formal complaints in order to pressure the parties to settle their differences, usually at the behest of the accused. In the process, it is not uncommon for the police to harass, intimidate, and abuse the complainant and her family.

The delay in registering FIRs has particularly detrimental consequences in cases of rape, assault, and battery because forensic evidence is critical for their successful prosecution; and forensic evidence, especially in sexual assault cases, is generally extremely transient. Since the police usually do not take a woman victim for a medicolegal examination to collect such evidence prior to registration of an FIR, the delay results in the loss of crucial forensic evidence and seriously undermines the prospect of securing a conviction in any subsequent criminal proceeding. For a full discussion of the process and mechanics of collection and legal role of forensic or medicolegal evidence, see the next section of this report.

Even after a woman victim of violence manages to register a complaint or FIR, her travails at the hands of an ill-trained, incompetent, and venal police force are far from over. For example, from victims and specialist attorneys we learned of numerous cases in which the police included incorrect facts and misrepresented the victim's narration of events in the FIR. In certain instances, the police had overstated the complainant's case by arbitrarily including false incriminating details; in others, the police had been negligent in inaccurately recording the complainant's statement; and in some cases, the police had tampered with the statement after reportedly receiving a payoff from the accused. This conduct causes serious problems as the legal process gets underway, because ostensible inconsistencies surface in the victim's subsequent testimony. Many victims are illiterate and fail to discern the discrepancies recorded by the police in a timely manner, and even if they do, it requires an arduous bureaucratic process to modify the report once it has been finalized.

In sexual assault FIRs, the police create further problems by failing to specify the applicable subsection of the zina law, hence creating ambiguity as to whether the charge relates to rape or consensual extramarital sex. Section 10 of the Offence of Zina Ordinance establishes the crimes of both zina (adultery/fornication) and zina-bil-jabr (rape) liable to tazir (discretionary punishment), and subsections 10(2) and 10(3) detail the tazir punishments for zina

---

[151] For a more detailed discussion of this problem, see Zia Awan, "Violations of Citizens' Fundamental Rights," *Dawn*, September 14, 1990.

and zina-bil-jabr respectively.[152] In registering FIRs in rape cases, often the police simply note "Section 10" charges without specifying whether the alleged crime relates to subsection 2 or 3; or at times they indiscriminately and incorrectly categorize all zina-related charges as Section 10(2) crimes. Not only does this change the focus of the subsequent investigation, trial, and sentencing, by mischaracterizing the charge against the accused; it also makes the complainant vulnerable to harassment or even prosecution, as will be discussed below.

The case of Raheela A.,[153] a young housewife who tried to register a complaint of rape with the Karachi police, illustrates several of the problems described above. Raheela A. was raped by two men who broke into her home in the Landhi area of Karachi on February 25, 1997.[154] In the course of the attack she suffered knife wounds and was briefly knocked unconscious when her head was bashed against a wall. Later the same day, after obtaining medical treatment, Raheela A. and her husband went to Sukhan police station in Karachi to file a report. Raheela A. gave her statement to the police, but the sub-inspector (SI) on duty discouraged her from filing a complaint and pressured her to forgive her attackers or to come to a compromise with them. The police kept Raheela A. and her husband waiting at the police station for two nights. "The SI kept stalling," Raheela A. told Human Rights Watch, "and finally registered the FIR on the third day" after she and her husband paid him Rs. 7,000 (approximately U.S. $140). Futhermore, the police incorrectly recorded the sequence of events narrated by Raheela A., which caused her subsequent testimony to be discredited for inconsistency.

Farida S. encountered similar problems when she tried to report the rape of her twelve-year-old daughter, Ayesha, by a distant male relative in 1996.[155] Farida S. went to the Race Course police station in Lahore on the day of the attack, but the police refused to record a complaint and instead advised her to reconcile with the accused. When she persisted, they asked her to produce the accused but turned her away when she offered to lead them to his house. The next day Farida S. returned to the police station, and this time a senior officer demanded a bribe of Rs. 5,000 (approximately $100). The FIR was finally registered another two days later when Farida S.'s employer (she worked in domestic service) intervened on her behalf.

---

[152] See the legal section of this report for more details.
[153] All victims' names have been changed to protect their privacy.
[154] Human Rights Watch interview, Raheela A., Karachi, May 15, 1997.
[155] Human Rights Watch interview, Farida S., Lahore, April 31, 1997.

Another case that highlights the obstacles encountered by women victims of violence to registering FIRs is that of Sajida M.[156] Sajida M. was raped in April 1997 at a house in Samnabad, Lahore, by her employer and two of his associates at the Karim Block Factory of S and T Trading. She told Human Rights Watch that it took her ten days to lodge an FIR regarding the attack at Gulshan-i-Iqbal police station in Lahore. Sajida M. and her family made repeated trips to the police station, but the station house officer (SHO) turned them away and was rude and uncooperative. After ten days, Sajida M. was able to approach a high-level official, a deputy superintendent of police (DSP), who was visiting the police station. The DSP ordered the SHO to record the FIR, but after the DSP left, the police made Sajida M. and her family members wait at the station all night before finally registering the FIR the next morning.

In another Lahore case, family members of Farhat K., a four-year-old victim of attempted rape, told Human Rights Watch that, when they tried to report the assault at their local police station, an assistant sub-inspector delayed registering the FIR for twenty-four hours and demanded and was given Rs. 1,000 (approximately $20) by Farhat's family to follow up on it.[157]

While many of the women victims we interviewed had been subjected to police demands for bribes, in all the cases except one the corrupt police suffered few consequences. Raheela A. was able to find a legal aid NGO to help her compel the relevant sub-inspector to return the Rs. 7,000 he had demanded; however, the sub-inspector was not disciplined in any way. In fact, Raheela A. and a member of the legal aid NGO assisting her told us that he orchestrated retaliatory action against Raheela's husband, detaining him in a police lock-up and robbing him of Rs. 11,800 (approximately $240).[158]

Registering complaints of domestic violence can be even more difficult than registering rape by a stranger, because, as a result of gender bias and a lack of training, the police almost always fail to recognize domestic violence as any kind of crime. In fact, the police see their role in these cases solely as that of mediator and routinely try to get the parties to reconcile. At times the police blatantly overstep their authority by drafting non-binding written settlements or agreements (*sulah nama*) between the parties. Although some victims of domestic violence who resort to police assistance may genuinely not wish to pursue formal charges, there is no justification for the police's generally discouraging all victims from

---

[156] Human Rights Watch interview, Sajida M., Lahore, April 14, 1997.

[157] Human Rights Watch interview, Farhat A.'s father and uncle, Lahore, April 15, 1997.

[158] Human Rights Watch interview, Raheela A., Karachi, May 15, 1997.

doing so. Demonstrating ignorance of the law, officers at the Lahore Women's Police Station told us that instances of minor beatings do not constitute a police case and that the police need register FIRs only in cases where the victim has sustained substantial injuries.[159]

The SHO of the Women's Police Station in Karachi echoed the comments of her colleagues in Lahore. She asserted that most domestic violence cases are civil in nature. She told Human Rights Watch that victims of domestic violence usually approach the police for consultation rather than formal intervention. According to her, the police's role is limited to counseling and mediation. "We call the husbands into the station and explain to them with love and affection not to beat their wives. They are good people, they listen. In order to get a reconciliation, I put pressure on the wives for balance, for otherwise the husbands will consider the process unfair."[160] Farzana Mumtaz, who works with Aurat Foundation, a women's NGO in Lahore, and has intervened on behalf of women victims of violence with the police, told Human Rights Watch that she was frustrated and her efforts thwarted by the self-appointed counselor role assumed by the police, which serves as a serious barrier to battered women seeking safety and justice.[161]

Harassment and Abuse of Victims

In addition to sabotaging women's efforts to prosecute their attackers, Human Rights Watch found that it was not uncommon for the police to harass, intimidate, and even physically abuse the complainant and her family members. The case of Rehana Z., a resident of the Mangopir area of Karachi, is a good example of the problem.[162] In early 1997 Rehana Z. was raped by two men who were aided by another man and a woman. Rehana Z. lodged a complaint at Mangopir police station, but her case was subsequently transferred to Assistant Sub-Inspector (ASI) Murid of S.I.T.E. (Sindh Industrial and Technical Estate) area police station.[163] The S.I.T.E. police came to Mangopir to pick up two defendants (one man and one woman); they also took Rehana Z. to the S.I.T.E. police

---

[159] See sections 332, 350 and 351 of the PPC. Human Rights Watch interview, Women's Police Station, Lahore, May 3, 1997.

[160] Human Rights Watch interview, Farrukh Sultana, SHO, Women's Police Station, Karachi, May 12, 1997.

[161] Human Rights Watch interview, Farzana Mumtaz, Lahore, May 2, 1997.

[162] Human Rights Watch interview, Rehana Z., Karachi, May 15, 1997.

[163] Although the S.I.T.E. police station is very far from Rehana's residence, her case was transferred there apparently because it houses a "women's cell" or specialized unit to handle crimes against women.

station—in the same vehicle as the two accused persons. During the ride, the accused threatened and verbally abused Rehana Z. At the S.I.T.E. police station, Rehana and the two defendants were kept in the same cell. Rehana Z. was kept at the police station overnight, although the male defendant was removed to a different cell for the night. A policewoman then slapped Rehana Z. and beat her with a wooden truncheon on her hands and the soles of her feet. Along with ASI Murid, she repeatedly pressed her to come to a reconciliation (*sulh, razi-nama*) with the defendants because, "Tomorrow you'll run off with someone else." The police also asked Rehana Z. for money for food and minor expenses (*chai pani*). She was dropped off at Mangopir police station the following day and released. Although ASI Murid was later suspended and a reinvestigation order issued due to the intervention of then-Sindh Chief Minister Liaquat Jatoi,[164] Rehana Z. said the police were proceeding with her case at a glacial pace and that any progress was due to continued pressure from the Human Rights Commission of Pakistan and a legal aid NGO.[165]

Farida S., whose case is described above, told Human Rights Watch about police misconduct during the investigation of rape charges filed on behalf of her minor daughter, Ayesha.[166] Shortly after Farida S. filed the charges, her house was attacked by the defendant's family members and she and her relatives were beaten. When Farida S. went to report the incident to the Race Course police station, the duty officer rudely dismissed her and told her to have a male relative speak for her. Farida S. had an exchange of words with the officer, who cursed and swore at her and threatened to detain her. When a male neighbor accompanying her offered to intervene, the police briefly took him into custody. The duty officer later briefly detained Farida S.'s two sons-in-law and filed minor criminal charges against her husband and two sons, one of whom was eleven years old. According to Farida S., the officer offered to drop charges against her family members if she reached a settlement in her daughter's rape case.[167] Finally, three months later, Farida S. appealed to a judge who dismissed the charges against her husband and younger son; her eighteen-year-old elder son was detained and granted bail about a month later.

---

[164] ASI Murid had closed Rehana's case, citing a lack of evidence and, falsely, the disappearance of the complainant. This prompted Rehana to approach the chief minister, who accordingly suspended Murid.

[165] Human Rights Watch interview, Rehana Z., Karachi, May 15, 1997.

[166] Human Rights Watch interview, Farida S., Lahore, April 31, 1997.

[167] Human Rights Watch was unable to contact the officer concerned to verify this information.

Human Rights Watch also spoke to women victims of rape who had been accused and detained on charges of adultery and fornication. Although police practice in this respect has improved over the past five years, the problem continues.[168] Zia Awan, a legal aid lawyer, told Human Rights Watch about the case of Sadia B., an Indian national who was raped by her Pakistani boyfriend and a couple of his friends in Karachi.[169] Upon reporting the incident to the Karachi police, Sadia B. was arrested and spent thirteen months in pre-trial detention on charges of zina until she was finally released on bail; her boyfriend was also arrested and detained but was released on bail after one month.

Jannat Khatoon, who spoke to Human Rights Watch at the Karachi women's prison, was abducted in 1996 to Nawabshah from Karachi and forced into marriage with a man who raped her repeatedly over several months. When she was finally located by her real husband and the police, she was taken to the Ibrahim Haideri police station in Karachi, where she was held for three days and beaten by a policewoman for "running away." Despite her protestations that she had been raped against her will, she was told that "the law is the law" and arrested for adultery. When Human Rights Watch spoke to her, she had already spent two months in pre-trial detention and, despite a few visits to the Malir District Court lock-up, had never come face-to-face with a magistrate or judge.[170]

Inadequate and Improper Investigations

In interviews with judges, human rights lawyers, prosecutors, and complainants, Human Rights Watch found that the police's performance in investigating registered complaints of sexual violence is extremely poor. In addition to failing to conduct timely and comprehensive investigations, including witness interviews, site visits, and forensic work, the police frequently use unprofessional and inappropriate investigative methods, such as interviewing family elders in lieu of eye witnesses or the accused, detaining family members in order to pressure witnesses or the accused to come forward, closing cases based on an oath by the accused or on behalf of the accused by family elders, and pressuring complainants to drop charges on the basis of such oaths. Furthermore, the police frequently embellish, modify, or incorrectly transcribe witness statements and sometimes even instruct witnesses to change their stories and include details that ostensibly support their cases. This makes it easier for the police to close and

---

[168] See Chadbourne, *Never wear your shoes.* Also see Human Rights Watch, *Double Jeopardy: Police Abuse of Women in Pakistan,* pp. 61-66.

[169] Human Rights Watch interview, Zia Awan, Karachi, April 23, 1997.

[170] Human Rights Watch interview, Jannat Khatoon, Karachi, April 26, 1997.

dispose of cases—and excuses them from undertaking a comprehensive investigation—because subsequent inconsistencies undermine witnesses' credibility and weaken cases in the eyes of prosecutors, magistrates, and judges. At times police tamper with witness statements after obtaining bribes from the accused.

The case of Farhat K., a four-year-old victim of attempted rape, illustrates the state of police investigative practice in sexual assault cases.[171] When Farhat K.'s family arrived at a Lahore police station on February 13, 1997, immediately after the attack, the police required them to rent a car in order to apprehend the accused. After taking the accused into custody, the police delayed registering an FIR and sending Farhat K. for a medicolegal examination for twenty-four hours; instead they mediated between the two sides to work out an informal resolution of the "dispute." When the negotiations failed, an FIR was filed. Before proceeding further, the investigating assistant sub-inspector (ASI) demanded and received Rs. 1,000 (approximately $20) from the complainant's family. The ASI's investigative work consisted of nothing more than taking statements from both parties in each other's presence. He then demanded that the complainant's family produce specific community elders to attest to the truth of their allegation and, alternatively, advised them to drop charges if similarly respected elders were to vouch for the accused's innocence. Since the complainant's family refused to go along with the ASI's proposals, the case was referred to the police station chief, SHO Malik Ashraf, who again pressured them either to "give an oath [of sincerity] or accept an oath [of innocence]." When Farhat K.'s family rejected these demands, the SHO reported them to a magistrate as posing a "threat to the peace" and asked for restraining orders, which require the posting of bonds, against a few family members on both sides. At this stage the investigation completely stalled.

Eventually Deputy Superintendent of Police (Defence Circle) Zaheeruddin Babar opened an inquiry into the facts of the case. The investigative procedure he adopted was equally unprofessional as that of the ASI and SHO Ashraf. Babar brought the parties together and instructed Farhat's family to nominate people, acceptable to the defendant's side, whom the defendant would then be required to bring forward to attest to his innocence. The purpose was to give the accused the chance to demonstrate that people known to both the accused and the complainant would give a *qasam* (oath of the accused's innocence). If the nominated people did not vouch for his innocence, then it would be understood that he was guilty.[172] When the accused's side failed to get any of the six nominated people to vouch for

---

[171] Human Rights Watch interview with Farhat's immediate family, Lahore, April 15, 1997.

[172] Ibid.

The State Response to Violence Against Women

his story by the appointed date, April 10, the DSP found for the complainant and the case was set to proceed, as Farhat K.'s family hoped, to the prosecutor. But, besides Farhat K.'s medicolegal evaluation, itself performed forty-eight hours after the attack, there was no indication that any further investigatory or evidentiary work would be undertaken by the police

Another complainant, Farida S., whose case is discussed above, told Human Rights Watch that the Race Course police took absolutely no action after registering an FIR for the rape of her minor daughter, Ayesha, despite the fact that the accused was known to be in the neighborhood.[173] After she made several trips to exhort them to investigate, the police finally accompanied Farida S. to her neighborhood, where she pointed out the accused at a roadside eatery. The police, however, took so long to park their vehicle that he easily absconded, and when Farida S. asked the police to make another attempt, she was told to have the police van refueled for the purpose. Moreover, a senior officer pointedly asked Farida S. for a bribe of Rs. 5000 (approximately $100). Throughout the process, the police constantly discouraged Farida S. from pursuing the case and pressured her to reach a truce with the defendant, at times taunting her that they would make no effort to investigate. They did not even take statements from the victim, Ayesha; Ayesha's younger brother, who was an eye witness to the rape; or Farida S.'s cousin, who saw the defendant leaving Farida S.'s yard, until two months after the incident when Farida S.'s lawyer, who knew the station chief, intervened. Other than Ayesha's medicolegal examination, conducted a few days after she was raped, that was the extent of the investigation.

The inertia and incompetence of police are compounded by pervasive corruption, as discussed above. Even judges have expressed skepticism about the quality and reliability of police investigations. Mian Khalid, a judge in Lahore, told Human Rights Watch, "The police officer writes wrong facts on the FIR, then the girl's testimony in court conflicts with that, and the case is thrown out. The benefit of any conflict or contradiction goes to the accused. Basically the police make a problem from the beginning by taking money."[174]

A Lahore prosecutor offered a related rationale for the police's mischaracterization of events:

> The police often implicate the accused's family members in the incident. Down the road contradictions emerge because of police fabrication. Also the police version often doesn't make

---

[173] Human Rights Watch interview, Farida S., Lahore, April 31, 1997.
[174] Human Rights Watch interview, Judge Mian Khalid, Lahore, May 3, 1997.

> sense, as when, for example, they assert that the accused's family sat quietly by while he committed the rape. The police implicate others because that way they can command more money [in bribes] and because they appease the victim's family who want the accused's female relatives to suffer because their girl suffered.[175]

Judge Javed Qaiser told Human Rights Watch that he concurred that the overall quality of investigations was abysmally low. "Police investigation is improper to the point that the families of victims want to withdraw charges just to escape police involvement. The police never gather evidence from the scene of the crime, and police bungling often makes it harder to secure convictions," he said.[176]

The police also routinely fail to fulfill their duty to process and handle any forensic medical evidence expeditiously. The transport of samples and other materials of forensic significance is the responsibility of the police; in Karachi and Lahore a policeman conveys samples in person from the medicolegal doctor to the government laboratory. However, samples are first taken to the police station where delays can occur before the sample is delivered to the laboratory. For example, a policeman interviewed by Human Rights Watch at the Office of Surgeon Medicolegal[177] in Lahore said that he would not be delivering the samples in his custody to the laboratory for another forty-eight hours because the following day was a holiday, and neither he nor the chemical examiner's staff would be working.[178] Similarly, another policeman we interviewed there on the morning of April 12 said that he would not drop off the samples in his care until the following day. Dr. Abbas at the Office of the Chemical Examiner in Lahore told us, "There is a requirement that all samples in any type of case in police custody should be sent to the lab within forty-eight hours. However, in practice, the police often delay."[179] The lack of police training in the handling of biological samples and the possibility of decomposition and contamination often render such evidence useless, especially in light of the fact that police stations are not equipped with the refrigeration and storage facilities sometimes necessary to preserve the quality of the samples.

---

[175] Human Rights Watch interview, district attorney, Lahore, May 3, 1997.
[176] Human Rights Watch interview, Judge Javed Qaiser, Karachi, May 15, 1997.
[177] The office of the chief of medicolegal services for Lahore and the central medicolegal examination center in the city.
[178] Human Rights Watch interview, policeman, Lahore, April 14, 1997.
[179] Human Rights Watch interview, Dr. Abbas, Lahore, May 2, 1997.

Medicolegal Examinations
Importance of Forensic Evidence in Cases of Sexual Assault and Domestic Violence

Medical evidence is central to the successful prosecution of both sexual and other bodily assault cases. The fact that in rape cases Pakistani courts generally require "positive proof of penetration"[180] as well as physical evidence, such as genital injuries,[181] to corroborate the victim's testimony as to the nonconsenual nature of the intercourse renders utterly indispensable a timely and meticulous medicolegal examination of victims as well as a sophisticated understanding of its merits and limitations on the part of courts.[182] In many cases of sexual assault, medical evidence may provide the only corroboration of the complainant's case, confirming not only the fact that sexual contact or intercourse took place—and with a particular individual—but also that such contact took place without the complainant's consent. Although medical evidence cannot in and of itself prove a lack of consent, it can be strongly suggestive that sexual contact or intercourse was the result of assault and not agreement. This is particularly important since, as discussed above, Pakistan's Hudood laws criminalize certain forms of consensual sexual contact: in many cases medical evidence may be the sole means for a rape victim to deflect the possibility of prosecution for adultery or fornication by demonstrating that the sexual contact in question was forced. Barriers to securing vital medical evidence not only prevent victims of sexual assault from mounting successful prosecutions and obtaining justice, but also heighten the potential for rape victims to be wrongfully prosecuted for adultery or fornication.

Medical evidence also plays a critical role in domestic violence cases: a medicolegal doctor's evaluation of the nature and extent of injuries determines the legal classification of incidents of domestic abuse and, consequently, the seriousness of the charges. However, concerns about the medicolegal system in the context of domestic violence remain largely theoretical because in the overwhelming majority of cases, the police simply do not conceive of domestic violence as a criminal matter, nor do they refer victims for medicolegal evaluations.

---

[180] There is no consistent standard for proof of penetration. Several cases, such as 1993 P.Cr.L.J 9 and 1993 P.Cr.L.J. 234 (PSC), seem to indicate that the standard is a broken hymen, while others, PLD 1989 SC 742 and PLJ 1989 SC 545 indicate otherwise.

[181] 1995 P.Cr.L.J. 241 (FSC); 1979 P.Cr.L.J. 575, 1979 L/Notes 310 (Lah.).

[182] In the absence of such corroborative evidence, courts usually accept the accused's version of events based on a general rule that the benefit of any doubt should always be accorded to the accused.

Nor do the police appear to be aware that a charge of criminal "assault" does not always require the victim to have sustained physical injury.[183] Since Human Rights Watch was unable to locate any domestic violence victims who were examined by medicolegal doctors, the remainder of this section will focus on the experience of victims of non-domestic sexual assault.

Despite the fact that criminal charges in cases of various forms of bodily attack depend on a medical determination of the nature and extent of injuries; despite the importance of medical evidence to securing convictions in rape cases; and despite the potential exculpatory role of medical evidence in adultery and fornication cases, Pakistan does not have an efficient and reliable medicolegal system. In general, medicolegal examinations are performed by poorly trained doctors using inadequate facilities and equipment. As bad as the system is for any victim of a violent crime, it has a disproportionately detrimental impact on victims of rape and sexual assault.[184] As a result, the government's maintenance and toleration of a deeply flawed medicolegal system is *de facto* discriminatory to women, who constitute the majority of rape victims.

Despite the potentially critical role for forensic evidence in rape cases, in practice, relative to victims of other violent crimes, women who have been sexually assaulted have to overcome particularly difficult barriers in order to get a medicolegal examination that yields any useful evidence. Rape victims must get authorization from the police and a magistrate's order before they can be examined by a government medicolegal doctor. These conditions may not seem difficult, but as the following subsections of this report show, in effect they serve to greatly delay and may even block victims' examinations. In addition, in most urban areas, rape victims can only be examined by a woman doctor at specialized state medicolegal centers. In contrast, most other types of cases requiring medicolegal services can be handled by the medicolegal units attached to most large

---

[183] See Sections 332, 350 and 351 of the PPC.

[184] There are several reasons for this. First, in contrast to other offenses, consent is a complete defense to the crime of rape; hence, evidence of *forcible* sexual intercourse is the *sine qua non* for a successful rape prosecution. Since it is generally rare to have eye witnesses to a rape, rape prosecutions are often a case of the defendant's word against the complainant's. In such a scenario, medical evidence would play a singularly critical role by indicating the occurrence and non-consensual nature of the intercourse at issue. A second factor that imparts a particularly important role to forensic evidence in rape cases is that the complainant's testimony in such cases is frequently devalued by biased officials. Third, rape victims face unique consequences if they are implicated in an unsuccessful prosecution: the possibility of charges of illicit sex, which also underscores the distinctive role of medical evidence in rape cases.

government hospitals.[185] This also becomes a problem in practice because of the shortage of female medicolegal doctors in government service and their limited hours of availability at a restricted number of state medicolegal centers.

Victims of violence face problems not only in the collection of medical evidence but also in its use in the courtroom. Our interviews with human rights lawyers, medicolegal doctors, prosecutors, and judges revealed that the examining doctors, prosecutors, and judges are not trained with respect to and have a superficial and simplistic understanding of the evidentiary scope and legal role of forensic evidence, especially in rape cases. Doctors present it in court without elaboration or explanation; prosecutors rarely question the doctors in order to elucidate its meaning; and judges treat the presentation of forensic evidence as a formalistic part of trials, do not subject the evidence to rigorous analytic scrutiny, and frequently misconstrue its significance.

Late Referrals and Other Police Delays

Sexual assault victims are entirely dependent on the police for information about and access to the medicolegal system. Most victims are unaware of the urgency, critical importance, or even existence of medicolegal exams, much less how to go about getting one. A victim cannot usually obtain a medicolegal exam on her own initiative. The medicolegal examination must, in practice, be done at a government facility for which an official police referral, police escort, and a magistrate's order are required.

It is generally advisable that forensic evidence be gathered and documented as soon as possible before time and intervening circumstances alter or destroy the signs and traces that constitute it. In cases of sexual assault in particular, it is critical that forensic evidence be obtained quickly because traces of semen not only disappear with time but can be lost through washing or passing urine. Other indications of sexual assault, such as internal bruising or swelling, are

---

[185] An assistant police surgeon at the police surgeon's office (state medicolegal center) in Karachi told Human Rights Watch that the provincial home department had recently issued a notification under which private doctors and hospitals could issue medicolegal reports for seriously injured patients under their care that could later be certified by a government medicolegal doctor upon reexamination of the accused. The notification did not appear to apply to victims of sexual assault. Human Rights Watch interview, assistant police surgeon, Office of the Police Surgeon, Karachi, April 22, 1997.

also often extremely transient.[186] Rather than promptly referring complainants for medicolegal examinations, the police appear to be unaware and unmindful of the urgency of medicolegal evaluations. They frequently delay or block women's access to this vital evidentiary evaluation, thereby compromising the chance of a successful prosecution from the start. The most common problem in this context is that the police, as discussed above, generally pay no attention to complainants until after an FIR is registered, and the considerable time and trouble entailed in filing an FIR automatically delays victims' medicolegal evaluations. Even after an FIR is filed, the police routinely neglect to secure prompt medicolegal evaluations for sexual assault victims. In some cases, the police have deliberately refused to provide referrals even to victims who affirmatively seek them. Often delays are caused because the police are ignorant as to the procedures to obtain an examination in sexual assault cases. In addition, the police undermine the preservation of forensic evidence by failing to inform victims of the need to refrain from washing themselves or their clothes prior to the examination.

Consider, for example, the case of Farhat K. described earlier, a four-year-old victim of a rape attempt that took place in Lahore in February 1997. Farhat K.'s family took her to the police station immediately after the attack to file charges. When they inquired about a medicolegal exam for Farhat K., the police said that it was not required for such a small child. When Farhat K.'s family insisted, and secured a taxi toward that end, the station chief persuaded them that an exam was not necessary. Although Farhat K. had not been washed or cleaned up following the attack, her family's repeated requests to the police to observe clear indications of the attack on her body were utterly ignored. The police changed their stance the following evening and took Farhat K. for a medicolegal exam, but no doctor was available. The next day, Farhat K.'s family made another attempt. Since they had been told that a magistrate's order was required, they requested the accompanying policeman to get one en route, but he insisted that it was not necessary. However, the doctor at the medicolegal center refused to perform the exam without the order, and Farhat K.'s evaluation was delayed for a fourth day.[187]

Parveen F., who had run away from home to Lahore, was raped by a man who had purported to help her.[188] She reported the attack to a police station the next morning on April 11, 1997. The police kept her at the police station all

---

[186] Some injuries, such as external bruising, may be more difficult to detect and evaluate immediately after infliction than several hours later.

[187] Human Rights Watch interview, Farhat K.'s father and uncle, Lahore, April 15, 1997.

[188] Human Rights Watch interview, Parveen F., Lahore, April 12, 1997.

day—while they undertook a preliminary investigation, arrested three suspects, and recorded an FIR in the case—and took her for a medicolegal evaluation that night. They were turned away by the staff at the medicolegal center because of their failure to obtain the required magistrate's order; they returned to the medicolegal center with the order the following day for an evaluation. The policewoman accompanying Parveen F. to the medicolegal center evinced ignorance as to the urgency or significance of medicolegal examinations in sexual assault cases.[189] She declared to Human Rights Watch, "It makes no difference when the exam is done; immediately or a month later, it is the same thing. Still, it is better that it proceeds sooner rather than later." When asked whether the police advise women to take any precautions to preserve evidence in instances in which an examination is delayed, she said, "We don't tell a woman not to shower or anything." As to the reason for getting an examination done, she asserted, "From the examination we can tell how many people have raped a woman. That is its importance." The policewoman complained that some victims' medicolegal evaluations are delayed because of difficulties related to obtaining the requisite magistrate's order. She said that magistrates are only available from 9 a.m. to 4 p.m., even though they are supposed to be available twenty-four hours a day, so if a victim comes to the police station after that time the police have to put off her medicolegal examination until the following day when a magistrate can be reached.

The case of Mehreen H., a rape victim in her early teens, handled by Officer Shamshad Abbassi of S.I.T.E. police station in Karachi, exemplifies the police's gross negligence with respect to medicolegal examinations of rape victims.[190] Mehreen H.'s father, who filed an FIR with the police on February 19, 1996, was told at the time that her medicolegal evaluation would be done a day or two later. Mehreen H.'s evaluation was actually done several days later because Investigating Officer Abbassi went on leave and did not arrange for it until after her return.

The experience of Kausar J., who was raped on April 28, 1996, was similar.[191] When Kausar J. filed an FIR at New Karachi police station on April 30, she was told that a medicolegal examination was required in the near future. Kausar J. returned to the police station three times over the next three days for this purpose, only to be turned away on one pretext or another each time. Her medicolegal evaluation was finally conducted on May 5.

---

[189] Human Rights Watch interview, policewoman, Lahore, April 12, 1997.
[190] Human Rights Watch interview, Mehreen H.'s father, Karachi, May 14, 1997.
[191] Human Rights Watch interview, Kausar J., Karachi, May 14, 1997.

Another rape victim, Raheela A., whose case was described above, told Human Rights Watch that, although she reported the rape to Sukhan police station in Karachi immediately after the attack in February 1997—before bathing or changing her clothes—her medicolegal evaluation was done three days later because the police, looking for a bribe, stalled on registering the FIR until then.[192] Sajida M.'s medicolegal examination was also delayed because the police took ten days to record an FIR in her rape case, which she reported on a timely basis after she was raped in April 1997 in Lahore.[193]

Inaccessibility of Doctors

After obtaining a referral, victims confront a second round of delays in getting a medicolegal evaluation owing to the frequent unavailability of medicolegal doctors. Unlike other assault cases, in sexual assault cases, in practice, only forensic evidence obtained by specialized state medicolegal offices [194]—in jurisdictions where they exist[195]—is admissible in court.[196] Although this is not mandated by law, most of the lawyers, NGO workers, and government officials we interviewed believed that this was the case; of the few who believed that evidence from other sources was admissible, many asserted that such evidence did not carry the same weight as that from state-run centers.[197] In fact, Judge Mian Khalid, citing the police rules and Law Department Manual, categorically stated that the testimony of private doctors was not valid in court.[198] Furthermore, most victims learn of the need for a medicolegal examination through the police, who routinely refer them to a government medicolegal center. Although the performance of medicolegal examinations of sexual assault victims is restricted to specialized state centers, even Pakistan's largest cities, Karachi and Lahore, with populations of

---

[192] Human Rights Watch interview, Raheela A., Karachi, May 15, 1997.

[193] Human Rights Watch interview, Sajida M., Lahore, April 12, 1997.

[194] The provision of medicolegal services is overseen by the departments of health of the various provincial governments.

[195] Specialized medicolegal centers exist in most cities and towns. In smaller towns and rural areas, victims of sexual assault are usually examined by staff doctors at the nearest government health facility.

[196] In domestic violence cases not involving sexual assualt, a victim could obtain an official evidentiary report from the medicolegal unit of a major government hospital.

[197] See Rehmat Bibi v. Muhammad Najib and another, 1997 P.Cr.L.J. 331, 336, cited in Chadbourne, *Never wear your shoes.*

[198] Human Rights Watch interview, Judge Mian Khalid, Lahore, May 3, 1997.

approximately eight and three million respectively, have only one such center each to service sexual assault victims from every part of their metropolitan areas.[199]

For many victims outside the central business area, simply getting to the one medicolegal center entails formidable logistical obstacles and considerable expense. While the police are required to escort the victim to the medicolegal center in a police vehicle, more often than not, police transport is unavailable. Rather the police direct the victim to hire a taxi, despite the usually long distances and consequently high fares involved.

Furthermore, medicolegal examinations of sexual assault victims at state medicolegal centers may be conducted only by female medicolegal doctors. All the medicolegal doctors interviewed by Human Rights Watch, including the chief of medicolegal services for Karachi, asserted that there was a severe shortage of female staff among the ranks of medicolegal officers throughout the country. Medicolegal officials in both Karachi and Lahore said that the medicolegal centers in the two cities are functioning with a minumum number of female doctors. For example, in Karachi there are only three women medicolegal officers (excluding a woman assistant police surgeon who does not regularly perform medicolegal examinations) covering the three daily shifts at the Office of the Police Surgeon (the government medicolegal center) and the government-run Abbassi Shaheed Hospital in the Nazimabad section of the city. Not only do these three doctors examine virtually all the sexual assault and adultery/fornication cases referred for medicolegal evaluations by the police, but they are also responsible for performing all postmortems on women. Officials at the police surgeon's office in Karachi consistently stressed the shortage of women medicolegal doctors and the consequent pressure on the three doctors currently on staff.

Although the medicolegal centers are theoretically operational twenty-four hours a day, women doctors are only available at specific times to perform evaluations in sexual assault cases. The scheduled hours of availability of a woman medicolegal doctor at the medicolegal center in Karachi are 9 a.m. to 3 p.m, six days a week. At other times and on holidays, a woman medicolegal doctor is theoretically available at the Abbassi Shaheed Hospital. According to doctors at the main medicolegal center, Abbassi Shaheed hospital was designated the venue for evening and night shifts of female medicolegal doctors because it is was more conveniently located with respect to their residences. The scheduled shifts for female medicolegal doctors at Abbassi Shaheed Hospital run from 3 p.m to 10 p.m.

---

[199] Although theoretically in Karachi sexual assault victims may also be examined at the Abbassi Shaheed Hospital, in practice, all such examinations are conducted at the central medicolegal center.

and from 10 p.m. to 9 a.m. However, medicolegal doctors at the police surgeon's office in Karachi and at Abbassi Shaheed Hospital told Human Rights Watch that the women doctors assigned to these shifts are not actually present on the hospital premises during their shifts. Rather, they spend the duration at home or elsewhere and remain on call; if a case requiring their attention is brought in, the male medicolegal officer on duty is supposed to telephone them.

In practice, however, sexual assault victims are almost never referred to Abbassi Shaheed Hospital for medicolegal examinations. Their only option is to go to the Office of the Police Surgeon between the hours of 9 a.m. and 3 p.m. on a working day. If a victim arrives at the police surgeon's office after hours, "If it is not a fresh case we ask her to come again the next day. If it's a fresh case, then we send her to Abbassi. . . . However, if it is after hours, the police usually wait till the following morning to bring women anyway—especially in rape cases."[200] It appears that the police are not informed about the option or encouraged to take victims to Abbassi Shaheed Hospital for examinations after 3 p.m. On the contrary, if the police bring a sexual assault victim to the police surgeon's office after 3 p.m. or on a holiday, in almost all cases the staff at the office, knowing that a female medicolegal doctor is not at hand on the premises of Abbassi Shaheed Hospital, tell them to return the next working day during the designated office hours instead of referring them to the hospital. Hence the potential availability of a female doctor to examine sexual assault victims at Abbassi Shaheed is essentially theoretical.

Based on the experience of victims interviewed by Human Rights Watch, female doctors are not reliably available at the police surgeon's office even between 9 a.m. and 3 p.m. As a result, many victims have to return repeatedly to the police surgeon's office and their medicolegal exams are delayed further. There is, for example, the case of Rehana Z.,[201] whose case was cited above, who was raped by two men in February 1997 in the Manghopir area on the outskirts of Karachi. Two days after the attack, on her second attempt, Rehana Z. was able to register an FIR. However, when she arrived at the police surgeon's office for her medicolegal examination—having hired a private car for the purpose and secured the required police escort—in the early afternoon that day, she was told to return the following day because the female doctor had left at 1 p.m. that day.

The medicolegal center for the district of Lahore is known as the Office of Surgeon Medicolegal, Punjab. Medicolegal evaluations for all cases involving

---

[200] Human Rights Watch interview, assistant police surgeon, Office of the Police Surgeon, Karachi, April 22, 1997.

[201] Human Rights Watch interview, Rehana Z., Karachi, May 15, 1997.

The State Response to Violence Against Women   71

a vaginal examination are performed by a woman medicolegal doctor there. Two female medicolegal doctors are assigned to the center. Between them they cover two shifts daily: one from 8 a.m. to 2 p.m., and the other from 2 p.m. to 8 p.m. Although the center is open twenty-four hours a day, no woman doctor is available between 8 p.m. and 8 a.m., and hence no medicolegal examinations of sexual assault victims can be performed during those hours.[202] A senior medicolegal officer at the Office of Surgeon Medicolegal noted that it was not enough to have only one female medicolegal doctor covering each shift at the center. When one of the doctors is called to testify in court, there is no doctor available to conduct examinations of women victims in sexual assault cases for the duration of the affected shift.[203]

Since a woman doctor is not available at night, and sometimes not even during the day, victims in Lahore also end up making repeated trips to the center, which often requires making special transport arrangements entailing substantial effort and expense. Furthermore, each trip to the center requires the victim to coordinate with the police to secure an escort, which can be difficult. Judging from victims' experiences, the police are ill-informed about the limited hours maintained by female doctors at the Office of Surgeon Medicolegal and sometimes take sexual assault victims to the center after hours when there is no possibility of their being examined. The case of Farhat K., the four-year-old victim of attempted rape discussed above, illustrates the problem. Farhat K. was summoned by the police to a Lahore police station at 8 p.m. on February 14, 1997 to be escorted to the Office of Surgeon Medicolegal for a forensic evaluation.[204] Farhat K.'s family, who lived on the outskirts of Lahore, hired a taxi for the purpose. They arrived at the center at 9 p.m., only to be told to return the following day by the male doctor on duty because no female doctor was present at that time. We interviewed Abida P.[205] while she was waiting for her medicolegal exam at the Office of Surgeon

---

[202] According to the staff at the Office of Surgeon Medicolegal, "For very big cases a lady doctor can be called from home during the night." Human Rights Watch interview, administrative staff, Office of Surgeon Medicolegal, Punjab, Lahore, April 12, 1997.

[203] Human Rights Watch interview, Dr. Akmal Shaheen, Lahore, April 14, 1997.

[204] Human Rights Watch interview, Farhat K.'s father and uncle, Lahore, April 15, 1997.

[205] Human Rights Watch interview, Abida P., Lahore, April 14, 1997. Abida P. was at the Office of Surgeon Medicolegal on April 14 to try to get a copy of her finalized medicolegal report. Although the police had taken her for a medicolegal exam, they had been refusing to register an FIR in her case. She was hoping that if she were able to get a copy of her report, she could take it to the office of the Inspector General of Police and ask

Medicolegal. She had reported a sexual assault to the police on April 9, 1997, and came to the medicolegal office the same night. Since no female doctor was available, Abida P. had to wait for a medicolegal evaluation until she returned to the center the next day.

Women in Pakistan's rural areas have virtually no chance of getting a timely or professional medicolegal exam. In most rural areas there are no specialized medicolegal doctors, and victims of violence must obtain medicolegal reports from the nearest government clinic or hospital, which often requires traveling considerable distances at substantial expense.

Victims of domestic violence potentially confront fewer barriers to securing a medicolegal examination if their injuries do not entail sexual assault. First, if a vaginal exam is not necessary, victims of domestic violence may be examined by male medicolegal doctors. Furthermore, these victims can be examined at any government hospital that has a medicolegal unit; there are several such hospitals in Karachi and Lahore. The medicolegal units at government hospitals are supposed to have at least one medicolegal doctor on duty twenty-four hours a day. Yet the theoretically greater ability of domestic violence victims to secure a medicolegal examination translates into little: they rarely get to this stage of the criminal justice system given the obstacles discussed above.

Lack of Training of Medicolegal Personnel

Although a post-graduate diploma course in "medical jurisprudence" is offered in Pakistan, the majority of medicolegal officers in the country, including those with supervisory responsibility, have no specialized training in the field of forensic medicine, either academic or practical, before assuming their medicolegal posts.[206] Human Rights Watch interviewed more than ten medicolegal doctors in

---

him to intervene on her behalf in this regard.

[206] Doctors assigned to medicolegal duties in Pakistan are drawn from a general cadre of doctors in government administrative service at the provincial level. From this general pool, the government appoints doctors to various medical positions, ranging from teaching in state medical institutions to working in assorted departments of government hospitals to holding medical posts in other state facilities such as prisons and medicolegal centers. Doctors in government service are categorized according to "grades" that are designed to reflect their levels of seniority. Government medical posts are classified by a corresponding system of grades: unless a post is classified as a technical or specialized position—and medicolegal posts are not—it may be filled by any officer who has the requisite grade or level of seniority. Medicolegal postings are highly coveted because of the perceived potential for corruption, graft, and personal gain.

The State Response to Violence Against Women

both the specialized medicolegal centers or headquarters and the medicolegal units of government hospitals in Karachi and Lahore.

To enter government service as a medical doctor, one must have a degree from an accredited medical college and a diploma in public health. Once inducted into government service, doctors are transferred from posting to posting over the course of their careers, which usually entails a corresponding change in the substantive nature of their duties. Hence, doctors find it difficult to build up specialized expertise in any particular field. Many of the medicolegal doctors interviewed by Human Rights Watch complained that there was little incentive to develop expertise in medicolegal work when they knew they could be transferred at any time. The doctors gave examples of colleagues who had been transferred to different positions shortly after acheiving a high level of skill in medicolegal work and who were replaced by total novices in the field.[207] The doctors also emphasized the fact that medicolegal postings were highly coveted and the appointments process very politicized because the field was perceived as having great potential for corruption, graft, and personal gain.

A senior medicolegal officer at the Office of Surgeon Medicolegal in Lahore, one of the few medicolegal doctors with specialized training in forensic medicine, told Human Rights Watch, "In this country there is no concept of training or specialization for medicolegal officers, most of whom are totally inexperienced. . . . Doctors don't have trained assistants either. . . . There is no system at all."[208]

---

[207] All but two of those doctors stated that they had acquired any medicolegal expertise they possessed on the job. Prior to their assuming medicolegal duties, most had little or no background in medicolegal theory and methodology except for a course in medical jurisprudence that is taught in the third year of medical college.

[208] This doctor mentioned that the Punjab provincial government had initiated basic medicolegal training at Lahore's Office of Surgeon Medicolegal for medical officers assigned to rural areas whose duties included medicolegal work. The training was particularly directed toward female medical officers in light of a recent Supreme Court ruling mandating that post-mortem examinations of women should be performed only by female doctors. However, as he described them, these training programs appeared to be fairly rudimentary, entailing brief apprenticeships with doctors conducting medicolegal work at the medicolegal office. Human Rights Watch interview, Dr. Akmal Shaheen, Lahore, April 14, 1997.

Dr. Lubna,[209] one of two female doctors on the staff of the Office of Surgeon Medicolegal in Lahore, and two of the three female doctors[210] on the staff of the Office of the Police Surgeon in Karachi told us that apart from a course in medical jurisprudence in medical college, the only training in medicolegal work they received was on the job. "I have training in gynecology and on-the-job training for this work," said Dr. Lubna.[211] A woman medicolegal doctor at the Karachi center told Human Rights Watch, "We learn by doing, by looking at book references and old cases, and by asking our senior colleagues."[212] Another medicolegal doctor at the Karachi center said, "There is no institutional or systematic training for medicolegal officers. We learn by consulting our seniors. There should be diploma training so that doctors have to pass an exam before they can work as medicolegal officers."[213] The doctors' assistants similarly receive no systematic training. In fact, several doctors reported that frequently janitorial staff ("sweepers") substitute for mortuary attendants, who assist doctors in performing post-mortem examinations.

This lack of training was revealed by the inconsistency we found in medicolegal doctors' knowledge of the need for a prompt medicolegal exam for victims of sexual assault. Some of the medicolegal doctors we interviewed even had incorrect information on the viability of sperm and tissue samples. According to Dr. Lubna, the urgency of the exam varies with the virginity status of the victim: "Unmarried women [i.e., women who were virgins before the assault] should have the exam done within ten to fourteen days of the assault" because the condition of a freshly torn hymen is best evaluated during this time frame. "Married women [i.e., sexually active women] can come within twenty-one days," because in these women, generally there are no discernable internal injuries in any case, she added.[214] On the other hand, Dr. Akmal Shaheen, a senior medicolegal officer at the Lahore office who does not examine women victims of sexual assault himself but serves as a resource for the doctors who do so, said that if a victim is examined two to three weeks after the assault, "the evidence is lost."[215]

---

[209] Human Rights Watch interview, Dr. Lubna, Lahore, April 12 and 14, 1997.
[210] Human Rights Watch interview, medicolegal doctors, Office of Police Surgeon, Karachi, April 22, 1997.
[211] Human Rights Watch interview, Dr. Lubna, Lahore, April 14, 1997.
[212] Human Rights Watch interview, medicolegal doctor (name withheld for confidentiality purposes), Karachi, April 24, 1997.
[213] Human Rights Watch interview, medicolegal doctor, Karachi, April 22, 1997.
[214] Ibid.
[215] Human Rights Watch interview, Dr. Akmal Shaheen, Lahore, April 14, 1997.

Doctors were also confused about the length of time during which semen may be detected in a woman's vaginal area. Dr. Lubna said, "For twenty-one days semen shows positive in the vagina, so there is no rush."[216] She does not take swabs if twenty-one days have passed since the assault because then, she said, the presence of semen cannot be detected by laboratory analysis.[217] Dr. Shaheen, on the other hand, said that while in a dead body sperm may be detected for up to three weeks for sure, and sometimes even for three months, in a live person the possibility of detecting semen depends upon a number of factors, including whether the woman in question is menstruating, has urinated, or bathed and washed herself. He said, although it was conceivable that sperm may be detected for up to seventeen days in the folds of the vagina, in general, motile sperm could be detected only within three to four hours of the assault. He felt that if a victim was examined more than seventeen days after the assault, there was no point in sending vaginal swabs for laboratory analysis for the purpose of detecting semen.[218]

Staff at the Office of the Chemical Examiner[219] in both Karachi and Lahore disagreed with both Dr. Lubna and Dr. Shaheen. According to a senior chemist at the Karachi laboratory, "Sperm can be found in the vagina for up to seventy-two hours [after the assault]. However, semen on clothing if properly dried and preserved may be detected for years."[220] The head of the semen section at the Lahore laboratory explained that "semen can be detected within three days [of the sexual assault]. However, in its non-motile form, semen may be detected for up to three months."[221] As for the process of semen grouping, which the doctors referred to several times though none knew of an instance when it had been successfully performed, Dr. Lubna said, "[It] can be done for twenty-one days after the assault without any problem,"[222] while Captain Memon asserted, "For semen grouping to be done, the girl has to come [for an exam] within twenty-four hours.

---

[216] Human Rights Watch interview, Dr. Lubna, Lahore, April 14, 1997. According to Dr. Lubna, a woman's bodily functions, including urination, have no bearing on the likelihood of semen detection.

[217] Ibid.

[218] Human Rights Watch interview, Dr. Akmal Shaheen, Lahore, April 14, 1997.

[219] These are the laboratories that analyze the results obtained by the medicolegal doctors. See more below.

[220] Human Rights Watch interview, senior chemist, Karachi, May 16, 1997.

[221] Human Rights Watch interview, Dr. Abbas, Lahore, May 2, 1997.

[222] Human Rights Watch interview, Dr. Lubna, Lahore, April 14, 1997.

After twenty-four hours sperms dissolve, although the presence of semen can be detected."[223]

The medicolegal doctors we interviewed said that in addition to a lack of training in medicolegal techniques and methodology, they receive no training in legal and testimonial procedures.[224] Doctors have no experience as to how to contextualize and interpret medicolegal evidence in a legal framework and testify with respect to it in a court of law. As a result, far from having a significant impact in cases requiring their testimony, medicolegal doctors perform perfunctory, formalistic, and superficial roles in the courtroom with their time on the witness stand reduced to a matter of minutes. The doctor's role is limited to reading out verbatim the medicolegal report they prepared and submitted to the court hearing the case. Doctors do not provide any meaningful explanation as to the limitations of the report or the range of implications of specific findings or lack thereof. They are present, in effect, merely to admit the medicolegal report into evidence rather than to provide the court with a comprehensive expert opinion as to the significance of the findings recorded in the report. Furthermore, several medicolegal doctors told us that usually cases take so long to come to trial, often up to a year or more, that by the time they are called upon to testify in a particular case, they have completely forgotten about it and just parrot their report, which is all they are expected to do in any case.

Several doctors specified that basic training in understanding a central element of Pakistan's criminal law, the Qisas and Diyat Ordinance, would be very useful. The Qisas and Diyat Ordinance aims to codify Islamic criminal law, and governs all crimes involving bodily injury including murder and assault but excluding sex crimes. It defines crimes and mandates punishments according to the nature and extent of injuries inflicted. The ordinance, which establishes fine distinctions between different categories of crimes and incorporates arcane Arabic

---

[223] Human Rights Watch interview, Captain Nizamuddin Memon, Karachi, April 22, 1997.

[224] Doctors at the Office of the Police Surgeon in Karachi also evinced confusion as to the procedural prerequisites for performing medicolegal examinations in cases of sexual assault and adultery/fornication, reflecting a need for the process to be systematized and clarified for the benefit of doctors and ultimately their examinees. The particular point of confusion was whether a magistrate's order is required before victims of sexual assault or women and girls charged with adultery/fornication can be examined. An assistant police surgeon at the police surgeon's office told Human Rights Watch that, although a magistrate's order was legally required in these cases—he showed us the relevant section of the police rules—the correct procedure was not followed in practice. Human Rights Watch interview, assistant police surgeon, Karachi, April 22, 1997.

terminology, has been consistently criticized in Pakistani legal circles and in the press for being extremely confusing.

Because of the ordinance's focus on the type and extent of injuries actually sustained by victims, the role of medicolegal doctors in identifying and documenting the injuries assumes great significance for the framing of criminal charges. In implementing their duties under the ordinance, medicolegal doctors not only need training in properly identifying and classifying victims' injuries, but also a thorough understanding of the scope of the ordinance and the numerous categories of crimes it establishes. While some medicolegal doctors we interviewed termed the ordinance's provisions confusing and difficult to comprehend and apply, others said that they had no problem precisely classifying victims' injuries with reference to the ordinance's crime categories.

Inadequate Equipment and Facilities

In order to be reliable and useful, forensic evidence must be collected, stored, and analyzed under sterile conditions. Ideally, tissue and fluid samples should help the police and prosecutors determine when and if sexual contact took place, whether there was a struggle, and with whom. The facilities at the medicolegal offices we visited did not meet these requirements and thus compromised the quality of the evidence.

Based on repeated visits over a four-week period to the premises of the Office of Surgeon Medicolegal in Lahore and the Office of the Police Surgeon in Karachi and on interviews with their staff, we found the physical facilities so inadequate that the performance of professional and thorough medicolegal evaluations was virtually impossible. Not only does the lack of equipment and amenities hinder the collection of forensic evidence, but it can lead to abusive treatment of the examinees, including exposing them to health risks. Some doctors also complained of feeling frustrated at their inability to perform their duties professionally and responsibly on account of the abysmal condition of their offices and the lack of proper equipment.

The Office of the Police Surgeon in Karachi is housed in dingy, dilapidated, and cramped quarters, with an atmosphere more like that of a prison than a medical facility. The examination room, which doubles as an office for the woman medicolegal officer (WMLO) on duty, is the smallest, darkest, and most stifling room in the building.[225] A WMLO told Human Rights Watch, "A patient

---

[225] A WMLO we interviewed informed us that, owing to her outrage at existing physical conditions, she had used her connections to get authorization for the construction of a new room at the police surgeon's office to serve as an office for WMLOs. The

who is already victimized will feel terrible in that room. A patient should be made to feel at ease and cared for."[226] This narrow, dirty, windowless and unventilated room has barely enough space to accommodate a cupboard, a small table, and a writing desk that functions as an examination table. This desk is wedged into one end of the room and is hugged tightly on three sides by walls, leaving the attending doctor to approach the examinee only from the side, along the length of the desk. The examination room is also very badly lit, with only one ceiling light and a small, unreliable lamp poised above the makeshift examination table.[227] This is very troubling because the goal of the examinations undertaken in the room often is to discern minute lacerations, fine cuts, bruises and discoloration on a woman's body, including her vaginal area, which requires strong lighting, particularly in the absence of specialized examination tools and equipment (See below).

Doctors performing medicolegal examinations on victims of sexual assault at the Office of Surgeon Medicolegal in Lahore and the Office of the Police Surgeon in Karachi are provided with virtually no instruments, or even supplies, to facilitate the identification and collection of forensic evidence. For example, doctors use wooden rulers to measure the dimensions of wounds on the examinees' bodies. While it is possible that a wooden ruler would suffice to approximate the surface dimensions of a wound, it cannot be used to measure its depth. A medicolegal officer at the Karachi office said, "We don't have proper kits to do [medicolegal] exams and post-mortems. I have never even seen a [examination] kit but have read about it in books. It should contain measuring tape, surgical knives, mirrors, hammer and chisel, and forceps."[228] A WMLO at the Karachi office told Human Rights Watch, "We have no torch, no forceps—zero equipment. The other day I had to buy a needle-holder for post-mortems myself."[229] During our visits to the medicolegal offices in Karachi and Lahore, there was no evidence of sterilized sample containers, optical examination aids, or other instruments of any kind, although X-ray facilities were available at the Lahore office.

---

examination room would, however, remain the same. At the time of our visit, the proposed office was under construction. Human Rights Watch interview, WMLO (name withheld for confidentiality reasons), Karachi, April 24, 1997.

[226] Human Rights Watch interview, WMLO (name withheld for confidentiality reasons), Karachi, April 24, 1997. The examination room affords no privacy to examinees, as one of its four walls stops a couple of feet short of the ceiling.

[227] Human Rights Watch interview, WMLO, Karachi, April 24, 1997.

[228] Human Rights Watch interview, medicolegal officer, Karachi, April 22, 1997.

[229] Human Rights Watch interview, WMLO, Karachi, April 24, 1997.

The State Response to Violence Against Women 79

Dr. Lubna, a WMLO at the Lahore medicolegal office, denied that the lack of equipment posed any difficulties for doctors: "There is no need for equipment since we do not have to give treatment [to the examinees]."[230] Similarly, when asked about the lack of equipment at the police surgeon's office in Karachi, Capt. Nizamuddin Memon, the chief police surgeon for the city, denied any shortcomings in this regard. "There's no instrument problem," he said.[231] However, the additional secretary of the health department of the Sindh government, which oversees the state's medicolegal facilities throughout the province, the capital of which is Karachi, conceded that the government provided "no proper equipment" and that there was a shortage of trained staff owing to lack of funds.[232]

In both the Lahore and Karachi offices, there is even a chronic shortage of disposable gloves, which are indispensable to a hygienic and thorough examination. This lack of basic supplies leads directly to abusive treatment of examinees, who are either examined with used gloves or required to purchase gloves for their own examinations. Uzma Saeed, a legal aid lawyer working with sexual violence victims in Lahore, told Human Rights Watch that on three occasions when she acccompanied a client to the medicolegal office she was told by the WMLO, "I don't have gloves. You have to bring gloves or give money for gloves."[233] A colleague of Ms. Saeed's at AGHS Legal Associates in Lahore recounted a similar experience,[234] and a WMLO at the Karachi office explained, "I sometimes ask the police to buy gloves."[235] Another WMLO at the police surgeon's office in Karachi told us, "Examination gloves are not meant to be re-used, but here they are re-used."[236] She said that after doctors finished examining a patient, they would throw the gloves used for the examination on the ground, and later these were rinsed, without even detergent or disinfectant, by the janitorial staff.[237] Health risks for both examinees and doctors are compounded by the fact

---

[230] Human Rights Watch interview, Dr. Lubna, Lahore, April 12, 1997.
[231] Human Rights Watch interview, Captain Nizamuddin Memon, Karachi, April 22, 1997.
[232] Human Rights Watch interview, Mr. Nawab, Additional Secretary (Health), Government of Sindh, Karachi, May 12, 1997.
[233] Human Rights Watch interview, Uzma Saeed, Lahore, April 14, 1997.
[234] Human Rights Watch interview, legal aid lawyer, Lahore, May 3, 1997.
[235] Doctors also complained that they were short of other basic supplies, including stationery, cleaning materials, and linen. Human Rights Watch interview, WMLO, Karachi, April 24, 1997.
[236] Human Rights Watch interview, WMLO, Karachi, April 24, 1997.
[237] Ibid.

that, according to a WMLO, female doctors have no access to proper washroom facilities, let alone bathroom access for examinees. Hence, the doctor added, it was difficult for doctors even to wash their hands. This is a particularly serious lapse given the intimate nature of the examinations performed by the doctors and the shortage of disposable gloves at the office.[238]

The lack of resources devoted to medicolegal services for women can also extend the delays that women experience in trying to obtain examinations. A WMLO told us that the fact that there was only one examination room means long waits for examinees, even if two WMLOs were present.[239] Examinations are also delayed by the periodic power outages that are common throughout Pakistan. A WMLO said, "Often the electricity goes. This room, already dark, becomes pitch black. Since there is no generator here, we have to wait for the electricity to come back on [to continue work]. Sometimes it is gone for hours."[240] The doctor elaborated that at times, if the power outage is prolonged or if the doctor's shift is coming to an end, examinees are sent back and told to return the following day.

Inadequate and Abusive Examinations: Sexual Assault Cases
Purpose of Medicolegal Examination

The purpose of medicolegal examinations of sexual assault victims, in theory at least, is to collect physical evidence related to the assault so as to help establish its occurence and the identity of the perpetrator. Moreover, medical evidence can be decisive as corroboration of a woman's allegation that intercourse took place without her consent, which, as discussed above, is particularly crucial in view of Pakistani laws that criminalize adultery and fornication.[241] The inadequacy of examinations in Pakistan contributes to the impunity with which

---

[238] Although we have no indication that a bathroom was included in the plans for the new WMLO office being constructed, we urge that the opportunity be availed to provide adequate washroom facilities for female doctors and their examinees.

[239] The doctors told us that most male examinees were attended to at the nearby Civil Hospital, Karachi. However, on occasions when males were examined at the police surgeon's office, the examination room used by the WMLOs was taken over for the purpose.

[240] Human Rights Watch interview, WMLO, Karachi, April 24, 1997.

[241] For nearly two decades, the government of Pakistan has vigorously applied its discriminatory and otherwise seriously flawed Hudood laws to prosecute women (and men) for adultery and fornication. Yet the government has made no effort during this time to update and improve medicolegal procedures that can provide vital exculpatory evidence with respect to the vast numbers of defendants who are wrongly accused of these crimes. See Human Rights Watch, *Double Jeopardy: Police Abuse of Women in Pakistan*, pp. 61-66.

violence against women occurs by making it extremely difficult to bring successful cases against those who commit sexual assault. It also further abuses women victims by subjecting them to sometimes dangerous and often humiliating examinations as well as making them vulnerable to criminal charges of illicit sex.

Though there is no single internationally recognized standard procedure for conducting medicolegal exams in sexual assault cases, many of the protocols that have been developed share most or all of the following elements:

- after obtaining the consent of the victim, the examiner takes a detailed history of the assault, including when and where the assault took place, whether the rape was anal or vaginal, whether and at what point during the assault the attacker ejaculated, and whether the attacker used a condom in the course of the assault;

- a thorough examination of the victim's body for visible injuries, including redness and swelling in the genital area and photograph each injury;

- collection of clothing that was torn or soiled during the assault and lab specimens, including saliva, sperm, blood, and any foreign object that could be used to identify the perpetrator (such as fibers, hair, dried semen) or the location of the assault (such as sand, fibers, and twigs).[242]

Furthermore, as recommended by the American College of Emergency Physicians, a thorough sexual assault exam must address the medical, psychological, safety, and legal needs of sexually assaulted patients and should include counseling about possible pregnancy and testing and treatment of sexually transmitted diseases.[243] Aside from physical findings and collection of laboratory samples linked directly to the assault, only gynecological information relevant to the the interpretation of the findings or laboratory data should be recorded.[244] Such evidence includes the date of the last menstrual period, any recent gynecological surgery, the number of

---

[242] See Linda E. Ledray, "Sexual assault evidentiary exam and treatment protocol," *Journal of Emergency Nursing, vol. 21*, pp. 355-359; Lee Madigan, *The Second Rape* (New York: Lexington Books, 1991), p.85-86; American College of Emergency Physicians, "Policy Statements: Management of the Patient with the Complaint of Sexual Assault," *Annals of Emergency Medicine, vol. 25, no. 5*, pp. 728-729.

[243] American College of Emergency Physicians, "Policy Statements: Management of the Patient with the Complaint of Sexual Assault," *Annals of Emergency Medicine, vol. 25, no. 5*, pp. 728-729.

[244] Ibid., pp. 54-56.

pregnancies and deliveries, and any consensual sexual intercourse within seventy-two hours of the assault.[245]

Pakistan has not formulated any official standard procedures for conducting forensic examinations of sexual assault victims. However, rather than centering on the collection of relevant evidence to establish the nature and extent of victims' injuries, the de facto focus of the examination is to determine whether she is a virgin. The exam is the same for both victims of sexual assault and women charged with illicit sex and involves the taking of vaginal swabs,[246] a quick check of the external genitalia for signs of redness and bruising, and a "finger test" and visual scrutiny of the hymen to determine its condition and the examinee's virginity status. In certain cases women are referred to laboratories where a urine test and ultrasound exam are performed to determine whether they are pregnant and, if so, the stage of the pregnancy. Some doctors may also take the initiative to elicit a history of events from the victim, but they are neither required nor advised to do so, and there is no standard protocol or list of questions for recording a victim's story. As a result, each exam is not tailored to corroborate elements of an individual victim's story; on the contrary, doctors perform a virtually pro forma examination on every examinee, whether she alleges rape or has confessed to adultery.

Inappropriate Focus on Virginity Status

There are several problems with the medicolegal doctors' focus on the condition—that is, whether it is torn or intact—of the hymen. This focus on the hymen has no legal or medical basis and instead reflects a misplaced preoccupation with the victim's ostensible virginity status and popular misconceptions about the medical verifiability of virginity. Modern medical standards hold that the use of visual scrutiny of the hymen or the "finger test"—another technique employed by

---

[245] Ibid.

[246] Dr. Lubna of the Office of Surgeon Medicolegal in Lahore said that three swabs are taken to detect blood and semen from the examinee's vaginal area; the swabs are sent to the Office of the Chemical Examiner from where one may be sent to the government serologist if required (see section on the Office of the Chemical Examiner below). In cases of attempted rape and also if the examinee's hymen is intact and penetration did not occur, "peri-vaginal swabs" or swabs from the external genital area are taken. "If the hymen is broken, then swabs are taken from inside [the vagina]," she explained. Human Rights Watch interview, Dr. Lubna, Lahore, April 14, 1997. At the Karachi Office of the Police Surgeon, in contrast, doctors prepare a glass slide with a vaginal smear, which is sent for laboratory analysis. Human Rights Watch interviews, two WMLOs, Karachi, April 24, 1997.

The State Response to Violence Against Women

medicolegal doctors in Pakistan—to make a determination of virginity status is highly suspect.[247] Nonetheless, these tests remain standard procedure in medicolegal examinations of sexual assault victims in Pakistan. The finger test entails checking the elasticity of the examinee's vagina by seeing how many fingers may be simultaneously inserted into the vaginal canal.[248] Nor is the state of a woman's hymen a reliable indicator of recent sexual intercourse and the nature, consensual or otherwise, of any such intercourse. The degree of elasticity, resilience, and thickness of the hymen, its location in the vaginal canal, and consequently its susceptibility to tearing and bruising, vary from person to person.

Furthermore, doctors do not simply record the virginity status of examinees on their reports; based on the finger test, they freqently make notations, such as "She is well used to sexual intercourse" or "She is habituated to sexual intercourse," that have no bearing on the issue of whether the defendant raped the victim on the particular instance in question. Such remarks about the sexual history of victims are then used by defense lawyers to discredit and attack their character at trial and potentially expose the women to prosecution for illicit sex.[249] Thus, the medicolegal report becomes a tool for defense lawyers by providing the basis for vilifying, retraumatizing, and stigmatizing the victim, which then serves to discourage other victims from pressing charges.[250]

---

[247] According to Dr. Greg Larkin, director of research, American College of Emergency Physicians, an expert in the field of forensic documentation of intimate partner abuse, there is no reliable test for virginity. Hymens can be torn by a range of common activities, and the presence of an intact hymen does not signify abstention from sexual intercourse. Human Rights Watch telephone interview, Pittsburgh, June 26, 1997.

[248] According to Capt. Nizamuddin Memon, "If only the tip of the little finger goes in, with a little resistance all around, then the girl is a virgin; if one finger is admitted, then she has had sex one time or casually; if two fingers go in, then the girl is used to it." Human Rights Watch interview, Capt. Nizamuddin Memon, police surgeon's office, Karachi, April 22, 1997.

[249] It should be noted that defense lawyers can bring in such clearly prejudicial evidence under Section 151(4) of Pakistan's evidence code, which reads: "when a man is prosecuted for rape or an attempt to ravish, it may be shown that prosecutrix was of generally immoral character." Furthermore, a 1997 Federal Shariat Court case held that "the rule laid down is that when a victim is proved to be a woman of easy virtue, her credibility is lost and no reliance can be placed on her testimony." *Muhammad Khalil, alias Kach v. State*, 1997 P.Cr.L.J. 1639, cited in Chadbourne, *Never Wear Your Shoes*.

[250] The Human Rights Commission of Pakistan has described this strategy of defense counsels in rape cases: "Offence thus often became the primary defence of the defence counsel who strained every nerve to sow doubt in the court's mind about the character of the victim. That practice was a principal reason for rape victims . . . to be averse

Finally, with their misguided focus on the examinee's putative virginity status, doctors virtually ignore other important aspects of evidence collection in sexual assault cases that could potentially corroborate elements of a victim's story, most significantly the non-consensual nature of the intercourse. For example, examinees are not required to undress fully for purposes of the examination, and doctors do not take adequate care in checking all parts of an examinee's body for bruises, scratches, bites, teeth marks, or other indicia of struggle or violence. In addition, doctors do not collect stray fibers or debris adhering to the victim's body that could be traced to perpetrators or the location of the assault.[251]

Dr. Akmal Shaheen, a senior medicolegal officer at the Office of Surgeon Medicolegal in Lahore, explained that the examination's focus on the virginity status of victims of sexual assault stems from the fact that Pakistan's rape law prior to the 1979 Hudood laws, as well as the Hudood laws themselves which now govern the crime of rape, established different penalties for raping virgins and non-virgins ("women used to sexual intercourse").[252] This rationale is, however, mistaken. The Hudood laws do not prescribe different penalties for rape based on the virginity status of the victim; rather, Hadd sentences for rape vary according to

---

to taking their complaint to a court." Human Rights Commission of Pakistan, *State of Human Rights in 1996*, p.126.

[251] It is possible that doctors refrain from collecting stray human hairs cohering to the victim's body or skin samples from under her nails that could be linked to the attacker because the technology for DNA testing and analysis is not available in Pakistan. However, at a minimum, they should fully examine the victim's body for any marks of violence or struggle, fibers that could visually be traced to a perpetrator, and clues relating to the location of the assault (e.g., carpet fibers or beach-sand particles). In addition to the incomplete physical examination of victims, there is no systematic procedure to collect and scrutinize an examinee's clothing from the time of the assault. In fact, among the medicolegal doctors and police we interviewed, there appeared to be a lack of clarity as to whether responsibility for the collection of clothing lay with the doctor or the police. Sexual assault victims interviewed by Human Rights Watch had differing experiences in this regard. Some victims said the police collected their clothing, others said that the medicolegal doctor checked their clothing, and the remainder said that no one had asked them anything about their clothing. One victim interviewed by us at the Office of Surgeon Medicolegal in Lahore immediately after her examination said that she had not washed her underwear since the attack but that no one had asked her anything about it. Human Rights Watch interview, Shaista B., Lahore, April 12, 1997. It is very important to check the clothing from the time of the assault of the victim and, if possible, of the defendant as well for any semen or blood stains or other materials from the location of the assault. Clothing samples should be carefully preserved until such time as they are submitted for laboratory analysis.

[252] Human Rights Watch interview, Dr. Akmal Shaheen, Lahore, April 14, 1997.

the marital, or, more accurately, muhsan[253] or non-muhsan status of the *offender*. Thus, there is no legal basis for performing the finger test on victims and recording conclusions regarding their virginity and level of previous sexual activity as opposed to an informed medical opinion as to whether penetration has recently occurred. Similarly, Hadd punishments for the crimes of adultery and fornication differ for muhsan and non-muhsan offenders. There is no sound legal justification for performing the finger test on women suspected of adultery or fornication, despite the distinction in sentences for muhsan and non-muhsan offenders, because the test cannot ascertain whether the examinee has previously had *legal* sexual intercourse, which determines her muhsan or non-muhsan status. Even if the test were legally relevant, it should be abandoned given its inaccuracy and inadequacy as a medical technique for its stated purpose of determining a woman's virginity and level of sexual activity.

The focus on the state of the hymen greatly reduces the value of the exam for all victims of sexual assault. Moreover, the uniform focus of and standard procedures applied in every examination renders it virtually useless for sexually active women for whom the patterns of injuries emanating from sexual assault can be considerably different from those of women who are not sexually active and hence require adapted examination techniques that take into consideration an examinee's age, whether she is sexually active, and the number of children to whom she has given birth. Many of the medicolegal doctors and law enforcement officials interviewed by Human Rights Watch acknowledged that the examinations of married women as currently carried out had little or no evidentiary value. Dr. Lubna from the Office of the Surgeon Medicolegal in Lahore said that in cases in which the victim was a virgin before the rape, the condition of the hymen is a useful indicator of recent sexual intercourse when the examination occurs in a timely fashion because it is possible to discern "a freshly torn hymen" and distinguish between "a freshly torn hymen and an old torn hymen."[254] "We can tell if the hymen is freshly torn with the eye, since it will have abrasions and lacerations around the edges. The edges of a hymen with an old tear are smooth," she said. She added, "For a married woman, one cannot tell if she has been raped or not from the hymen. Also, no injury shows, especially in older women, so generally not much evidence is collected from married women. . . . It helps in the

---

[253] Section 2 of The Offence of Zina (Enforcement of Hudood) Ordinance, 1979, defines muhsan as "a Muslim adult man [woman] who is not insane and has had sexual intercourse with a Muslim adult woman [man] who, at the time he [she] had sexual intercourse with her [him], was married to him [her] and was not insane."

[254] Human Rights Watch interview, Dr. Lubna, Lahore, April 12, 1997.

case of unmarried women that the vagina is tight, to show that it could have been rape."[255]

The police do not expect medicolegal exams of married women to be useful in terms of securing evidence because of the focus on the condition of the hymen. SHO Ashiq Martha of Ichra police station told Human Rights Watch, "In the medicolegal exam, doctors check women's chastity. If it is a virtuous and pure woman, her body will have changed. So for virgins, because the internal hymen tears, the medicolegal exam is useful. For married women, no internal wounds are possible. Only external bodily injuries can be found."[256] Judge Javed Qaiser also asserted that medicolegal exams of married women were not effective. "The [condition of the] hymen is the only way to determine [for virgin victims] what occurred, though hymens can also be broken by activities like cycling. But for married women, how can medical exams help?" he asked.[257] A WMLO at the police surgeon's office in Karachi had an answer. She said,"If a woman has been married for a while, there will still be congestion [redness], though only for a day or two. We can find vaginal injuries, but time is of the essence. Also, if the woman has struggled, we can find signs of struggle on other parts of the body such as the breasts, thighs, swollen lips."[258]

Haphazard Procedures

The fact that doctors do not even consistently ask victims for details about the assault also undermines an exam's value because, in order to be comprehensive and elucidative, the exam should reflect and be informed by the victim's experience. In part because of the mistrust and skepticism discussed earlier, medicolegal doctors examining victims of sexual assault in Pakistan as a rule conduct exams and seek evidence strictly in accordance with written police requests and as ordered by a magistrate.[259]

Some doctors pointedly refrain from asking the victim her story. Others, we found, interrogate the victim with a view to demonstrating the purported implausibility of her version of events. Three Karachi doctors we interviewed try to take a history of the incident from the examinee unless the information provided

---

[255] Ibid.

[256] Human Rights Watch interview, Station House Officer Ashiq Martha, Lahore, April 14, 1997.

[257] Human Rights Watch interview, Judge Javed Qaiser, Karachi, May 15, 1997.

[258] Human Rights Watch interview, a senior WMLO, Karachi, April 24, 1997.

[259] Human Rights Watch interview, Dr. Lubna, Lahore, April 14, 1997; Human Rights Watch interviews with several examinees, Lahore, April 12-14, 1997.

by the police is satisfactory;[260] however, they have not been provided with a systematized protocol or list of questions and do not, for example, ask questions about condom usage or ejaculation by the defendant. Dr. Lubna explained, "We don't take a history from the woman because she could fabricate or say what her parents have told her to say."[261] Dr. Lubna does not use a standard list of questions to elicit information about the assault from examinees: "It would not help if we used a questionaire because we would not know if the woman is telling the truth or not."[262] The doctor said that the exam procedure includes checking the virginity of unmarried women to "[s]ee if she is lying and is actually habituated to sex."[263] She added that it was important to match any semen found on an examinee's body with that of the defendant because "[s]he could have put someone else's semen on herself" to frame the defendant.[264] It appears that Dr. Lubna views a medicolegal examination primarily as a means of discrediting a rape victim's testimony rather than an objective evidentiary procedure.

The legal importance of a proper and thorough medicolegal examination is underscored by the evidentiary criteria established by Pakistan's rape laws, which require proof of penile penetration as well as corroboration of a woman's allegation of rape. In light of these requirements, the inadequacy of existing examination procedures is particularly glaring. Medical evidence is generally indispensable to prove penetration in particular, since it is extremely rare to have eye witnesses to the act of penetration. Given that medicolegal doctors acknowledge that the current examination techniques frequently do not uncover significant evidence in "married" or sexually active women to prove penetration or corroborate an allegation of rape, the scales of justice are tipped against these women victims even before they step into the courtroom.

Mistreatment of Victims

As Doctor Lubna's derisive and incredulous attitude towards examinees described above indicates, victims arriving at the Office of Surgeon Medicolegal in Lahore are often treated harshly and insensitively by medicolegal staff. Reflecting a similar situation, doctors at Karachi's main medicolegal center spoke to Human Rights Watch of outright harrassment of female examinees by the chief

---

[260] Human Rights Watch interviews, Dr. Aftab, Karachi, April 22, 1997, and two WMLOs, Karachi, April 24, 1997.
[261] Human Rights Watch interview, Dr. Lubna, Lahore, April 12, 1997.
[262] Human Rights Watch interview, Dr. Lubna, Lahore, April 14, 1997.
[263] Ibid.
[264] Ibid.

police surgeon for Karachi, Capt. Nizamuddin Memon. In fact, when our researcher interviewed him for this report, Captain Memon broached inappropriate topics related to prostitution and various sexual practices that were not relevant to the purposes of the interview. His unprofessional conduct during the interview coincided with his colleague's descriptions of his behavior in the course of fulfilling his duties, which include examining women to determine their ages based on an assessment of signs of puberty.[265] When we interviewed him, Dr. Memon expressed an unwaveringly oppositional attitude toward victims of rape: "WMLOs have experience and can tell if a woman has been genuinely raped or not. Since September 1996 [when he assumed the post of chief police surgeon] there have been only two cases of genuine rape. Others come in the hundreds, but they lie. Those are zina [adultery/fornication] cases. Rape victims do not report attacks based on social factors."[266] Although Capt. Memon's behavior might be an extreme example of abuse of authority, there is no doubt that the criminalization of adultery and fornication serves to create an environment in which all examinees are routinely humiliated and mistreated.

Another manifestation of medicolegal doctors' lack of sensitivity to the needs of sexual assault victims is that doctors do not inform victims, regardless of

---

[265] Age assessments are done for women who have been accused of adultery or fornication since, under the Hudood Ordinances, a woman is considered to have attained the age of majority upon puberty.

[266] Human Rights Watch interview, Capt. Nizamuddin Memon, Karachi, April 22, 1997. During the interview Captain Memon gave an example that he believed supported his claims that women alleging rape are liars:

> The police brought a thirteen- or fourteen-year-old girl to be examined who claimed she had left home because her brother had raped her three times. However, her brother had reported her missing to the police. I questioned the girl regarding her whereabouts. She said that she took refuge with an old man and his family whom she met at a bus stop and that when she saw a story in *Awam* newspaper that said that she had been abducted and a police report had been filed concerning the case, the old man took her back to the bus stop so that she could go to the police herself. I did not believe her, because how could the old man have brought her to the bus stop in plain view [*khullay aam*] when a story about her had appeared in the paper? The girl was lying.

He also stated that some examinees alleging rape were sent for pregnancy tests to make sure that they were not lying about events: "We do this because sometimes the girl has been missing for one week only but the pregnancy turns out to be two months old."

their age, of the nature of the examinations or take any other steps to minimize the intimidation associated with the examinations. The women we interviewed in both Lahore and Karachi were not told, for example, what samples would be taken or to what purpose they would be taken, nor were the doctors' preliminary findings explained to them following the examination.

Finally, it should be noted that apart from referrals for pregnancy tests provided by the Karachi medicolegal center, medicolegal doctors fail to provide victims of sexual assault with even minimal treatment for the health consequences of the attack. In the words of Dr. Lubna of the Office of Surgeon Medicolegal in Lahore, "Treatment is not our concern."[267] Although in cases of serious injury, doctors do refer women to government hospitals where they can obtain treatment, in most cases the medicolegal doctor is the only doctor a victim of assault will see. Hence, the failure to provide basic counseling and treatment is particularly troubling.

Inadequate and Abusive Exams: Adultery or Fornication Cases

In Pakistan, the same doctors perform examinations on both victims of sexual assault and women accused of adultery or fornication. The doctors examine many more women in the latter category than in the former. As difficult as the exam may be for a victim of sexual assault, women accused of adultery confront doctors who are even less sympathetic. The doctors' skepticism towards their examinees is sometimes colored by the misguided perception that they are criminals and "wayward" women. This perception not only violates the professional objectivity expected from a doctor but also denies women their right to the presumption of innocence, since women charged with adultery or fornication are taken for medicolegal examinations prior to trial and many women are wrongly accused of these crimes.[268]

Captain Nizamuddin Memon, the chief police surgeon and head of medicolegal services for metropolitan Karachi, exemplified the hostility with which women and girls accused of adultery or fornication are treated:

> The day before yesterday, the police brought a zina [fornication] case to our office. The girl was screaming and not letting the lady doctor touch her, acting as if the exam was too painful. Finally the accompanying policewoman had to hit her and

---

[267] Human Rights Watch interview, Dr. Lubna, Lahore, April 12, 1997.
[268] See Human Rights Watch, *Double Jeopardy: Police Abuse of Women in Pakistan*, pp. 61-66.

persuade her to have the exam. When the doctor did the exam, the girl's vagina admitted two fingers. So how [in light of the elasticity of the vagina] could the exam have been painful? Clearly the girl had been tutored to make a noise even at the touch of a finger so that she appeared to be a virgin . . . If the vagina admits two fingers, then the girl is used to sex.[269]

As the above example shows, examinations of women charged with adultery or fornication can also turn abusive when they are performed without the consent of the woman involved. According to the police rules, when the police request a vaginal medicolegal exam of a female, they must first take the potential examinee before a magistrate, who issues an order for the exam if she consents. At the Office of the Police Surgeon in Karachi, however, this procedure is routinely ignored, and doctors conducting the exams are not even aware of the rule.[270] In some instances examinations are performed in the face of express reluctance on the part of examinees. Nazia D., an eighteen-year-old woman charged with fornication, was interviewed by Human Rights Watch while in pre-trial detention at Lahore Central Jail.[271] Nazia D. was picked up by the police and taken to Baghbanpura police station after her mother filed a complaint of illicit sex. The police took her to a magistrate who recorded her statement but did not ask whether she would consent to a medicolegal exam. Thereafter she was kept at Baghbanpura police station for three days, after which she was taken for a medicolegal exam. When she told the police that she did not want one, the escorting policeman said, "You will have both the exam and a beating."[272] The examining doctor proceeded with the exam without Nazia D.'s consent. When Nazia D. made clear that she did not want the exam done, the doctor said, "I have to do what I am told." Subsequently, when she was brought back to the police station lock-up, the police beat her with shoes for having attempted to refuse the medicolegal exam.

Role of the Office of the Chemical Examiner

Pakistan's two main governmental analytical laboratories, known as the Office of the Chemical Examiner, are located in Karachi and Lahore and are

---

[269] Human Rights Watch interview, Dr. Nizamuddin Memon, Karachi, April 22, 1997.

[270] Human Rights Watch interview, assistant police surgeon, Office of the Police Surgeon, Karachi, April 22, 1997.

[271] Human Rights Watch interview, Nazia D., Lahore, April 14, 1997.

[272] Ibid.

The State Response to Violence Against Women

overseen by the departments of health of the Sindh and Punjab governments respectively. These laboratories provide toxicological and biological forensic expertise for large swaths of the country. The Karachi laboratory, for instance, services all of lower Sindh and the entire province of Balochistan.

According to doctors, lawyers, and judges interviewed by Human Rights Watch, the test results and analysis reports from both the Karachi and Lahore laboratories were not always reliable, largely as a result of corruption and incompetence in the ranks of the laboratory staff.[273] Dr. Akmal Shaheen asserted that he had occasionally questioned personnel at the chemical examiner's office in Lahore when he received unexpected results for certain tests and was told, "Our petri dishes are contaminated."[274] Though these problems affect all cases that involve forensic evidence, they are particularly devastating to the prosecution of sexual assault cases, in which corroborating forensic evidence is crucial.

Laboratory staff explained that their ability to obtain accurate results was often limited by the condition of the samples that they received. They complained that sometimes samples are improperly or inadequately labeled, contaminated, decomposed, or otherwise damaged.[275] But the quality of test results also suffers from incompetence and corruption at the laboratories themselves. Like the medicolegal doctors, the staff at the Office of the Chemical Examiner are insufficiently trained for their responsibilities. Although graduate degree and diploma courses in toxicology, clinical pathology, and medical jurisprudence are offered in Pakistan, the staff we interviewed at both the Karachi and Lahore laboratories said that they received no specialized training to enable them to do their jobs, nor was such training a prerequisite for being hired for their positions.[276] Untrained people also hold supervisory positions in the chemical examiner's office,

---

[273] In sexual assault cases, the chemical laboratories test vaginal swabs or slides for the presence of semen. The semen section of the Lahore laboratory receives three vaginal swabs taken by the examining medicolegal doctor, while that of the Karachi laboratory receives a single slide with a vaginal smear. The laboratories generally use optical techniques to detect the presence of semen.

[274] Human Rights Watch interview, Dr. Akmal Shaheen, Lahore, April 14, 1997.

[275] Human Rights Watch interview, Dr. Abbas, supervisor, semen section, Lahore chemical examiner's office, Lahore, May 2, 1997; Human Rights Watch interviews, semen department staff, Office of the Chemical Examiner, Karachi, May 16, 1997.

[276] Human Rights Watch interviews, Dr. Abbas and Dr. Mahir Shah, Lahore, May 2, 1997; Human Rights Watch interviews, semen department staff, Office of the Chemical Examiner, Karachi, May 16, 1997.

despite government regulations requiring some technical qualifications.[277] Even if accurate test results are obtained, delays at the laboratories can render such evidence useless. According to a senior chemist at the Chemical Examiner's Office in Karachi, the laboratory takes one-and-a-half months at a minimum to generate a semen analysis report. "It can take three months or more," she said. As for the work load at the laboratory's semen section, she said. "Per month about twenty to twenty-five cases come to the semen section."[278] Additional Sessions Judge Javed Qaiser complained that delays at the chemical examiner's office routinely held up cases and pointed to corruption as the cause of the problem. "Usually the chemical examiner's report is so delayed that even the witnesses and parties have given up on the case. So even if the report is favorable, it is no use . . . The police surgeon's reports arrive relatively on time. The chemical examiner takes years, and cases get stuck. This is a monumental problem. There is a lot of corruption in that office."[279] Similarly, Islamuddin Ayubi, an assistant public prosecutor in Karachi, said, "The chemical examiner's report takes time; sometimes it doesn't come at all. We have to call for it repeatedly. Usually it takes a minimum of six months. The police should pursue the chemical examiner more vigorously for the report."[280] A lawyer with a legal aid NGO for rape victims in Karachi told us, "In 90 percent of our cases, there is no sign of the chemical examiner's report."[281]

Use of Medical Evidence at Trial

In sexual assault cases, the report of the medicolegal doctor, which is generally prepared within twenty-four hours of the examination of a victim, is admitted into evidence, and the doctor is required to testify in court regarding the examination and her findings. The doctor's testimony is usually based directly on the report. In Karachi, the chief chemical examiner also testifies in court as to the

---

[277] Reflecting a lack of training in forensics, when we asked Dr. Liaquat, the Chief Chemical Examiner for Karachi, whether his laboratory receives tissue or clothing samples of women victims of intentional burning (fire or acid), he responded, "What do we have to do with that?" Human Rights Watch interview, Dr. Liaquat, Karachi, April 29, 1997. When prompted that it would be important to check such samples for the presence of acid or kerosene, he said, "The woman's statement is enough. Moreover, you can tell if kerosene is present from the smell from the victim."

[278] Human Rights Watch interview, a senior chemist (name withheld on request), Office of the Chemical Examiner, May 16, 1997.

[279] Human Rights Watch interview, Judge Javed Qaiser, Karachi, May 15, 1997.

[280] Human Rights Watch interview, Islamuddin Ayubi, assistant public prosecutor, District West (Karachi), Karachi, May 15, 1997.

[281] Human Rights Watch interview, legal aid lawyer, Karachi, May 15, 1997.

findings in the analysis reports prepared by his staff,[282] while in Lahore, the findings of the Office of the Chemical Examiner are simply incorporated into the doctor's medicolegal report, and none of the laboratory staff testifies.[283]

Lawyers and judges interviewed by Human Rights Watch complained that doctors and chemical examiners frequently failed to appear in court when summoned to do so and hence further delayed the progress of already slow-moving cases. Rashida Patel, a Karachi lawyer, gave an egregious—but not atypical—example: a 1992 case that was still pending in May 1997. "The case is at its final stage. All the evidence is in. The examination of witnesses was completed by the end of 1996, except for the chemical examiner and the medical doctor. They have been summoned for the past six months but have not appeared. That's all we're waiting for."[284]

Even more disturbing is the fact that medical evidence, as it is currently collected, presented, and interpreted, often provides little assistance to the prosecutor and may instead serve to humiliate and even incriminate the victim. Referring to the unhelpful substantive format of medicolegal reports in rape cases, Karachi prosecutor Islamuddin Ayubi noted, "[t]he chemical report that records the presence of semen is more important for the prosecution than the medicolegal report."[285] This is a problematic conclusion in its own right since penetration, without ejaculation, is sufficient to constitute rape under Pakistani law. Judge Javed Qaiser concurred with Ayubi's unfavorable assessment of the medicolegal report, telling Human Rights Watch that a finding of lack of consent in a rape case usually hinged on circumstantial rather than medical evidence.[286]

Doctors' poor presentation in court, lack of training, and the present focus of the medicolegal report on the virginity status of the victim turn these exams into an effective tool for the defense case. Defense lawyers aggressively use the medicolegal doctor's stated findings to their advantage. Any notations in the medicolegal report, such as "She is used to sexual intercourse" or "She is habitual," are seized upon by defense counsel to smear the character of the victim. As a result, it is not uncommon to find the phrase, "a woman of easy virtue," with

---

[282] Human Rights Watch interview, Dr. Liaquat, Chief Chemical Examiner (Karachi), Karachi, April 29, 1997.

[283] Human Rights Watch interviews, Office of the Chemical Examiner staff, Lahore, May 2, 1997.

[284] Human Rights Watch interviews, Rashida Patel and her assistant, Farida, Karachi, May 16, 1997.

[285] Ibid.

[286] Human Rights Watch interview, Judge Javed Qaiser, Karachi, May 15, 1997.

reference to the victim in judicial opinions in sexual assault cases.[287] Judge Mian Khalid told Human Rights Watch, "In rape cases, male [defense] lawyers question the victim and her family in a terrible way, asking all kinds of crude questions . .

Judges get intimidated and cannot control the questioning. The standard of lawyers is very low."[288] Similarly, a district attorney (prosecutor) in Lahore told us:

> The atmosphere in court in such cases is very hostile to women, even to the lady doctors who are there to testify. The past sexual history of the victim is thrown around and touted in court to the maximum. Not only is the term "habitual" used to make the victim seem bad but the character of other women in her family is questioned. The lady doctor is pressed by the defense to explain the meaning of the term "habitual" to the point that it becomes embarassing and she finds it difficult to testify.[289]

The prosecutor's examination of the medicolegal doctor is, on the contrary, formalistic and cursory. According to Hina Jilani, a leading human rights and criminal lawyer, generally it is devoid of any attempt to grapple with the issues raised by the report, is very brief, and has minimal impact on the judge's understanding and consideration of the medical evidence.[290] There is a dire and immediate need for training in the interpretation and implications of medical evidence for prosecutors.

---

[287] See Chadbourne, *Never Wear Your Shoes*. The practice of assessing the level of sexual activity of victims in medicolegal reports and the effect on judges is particularly disturbing in light of legal precedents that have held, for example, "Once it is found that the prosecutrix had indulged in sexual intercouse previously also, her statement loses weight and her statement has to be looked [at] with caution and unless corroborated in material particulars cannot be made the basis of conviction." *Manhoob Hussain v. State*, PLD 1988 FSC 3, cited in Chadbourne, *Never Wear Your Shoes*.

[288] Human Rights Watch interview, Judge Mian Khalid, Lahore, May 3, 1997.

[289] Human Rights Watch interview, district attorney, Lahore, May 3, 1997.

[290] Human Rights Watch interview, Hina Jilani, Lahore, April 11, 1997.

VII. THE RESPONSE OF THE INTERNATIONAL COMMUNITY

Pakistan is an active member of several international and regional consortia, including the U.N., the Organization of Islamic Conference, and the South Asian Association for Regional Cooperation. In addition, Pakistan works continually to maintain and improve its bilateral relationships with its neighbors and donor countries. Pakistan receives about U.S.$2 billion per year from bilateral donors and international financial institutions. Much of this assistance comes in the form of loans, debt restructuring, and direct investment. Pakistan has an external debt of $28.6 billion and regularly has both a budget and a trade deficit. The government has been actively pursuing increased direct investment in order to lessen its dependence on foreign loans and grants. Assistance that comes in the form of grants often goes toward infrastructure improvements and finance reform, with little for programs that will directly affect women. Several donor countries and multilateral institutions have "women in development" programs or policies, but few such programs are being administered in Pakistan. Those that exist do not directly address violence against women or the inadequate response of the government.

The United States

Following the Soviet invasion of Afghanistan, the U.S. rewarded Pakistan's support of the Afghan resistance and its hosting of Afghan refugees with renewed aid. During the 1980s, the U.S. provided more than $7 billion in military and economic assistance. All military and new economic assistance was halted in October 1990 under a U.S. law that forbids non-emergency aid to countries that possess nuclear devices.[291] Since then, Pakistan has continued to receive some emergency assistance from the U.S., primarily for its Afghan refugee population, and the two countries have worked together to prevent drug trafficking and weapons proliferation in the region.

In March 1995 First Lady Hillary Clinton included Pakistan in her tour of Asia, signaling improving relations between the U.S. and Pakistan. In a November 1997 trip to South Asia, Secretary of State Madeleine Albright announced the

---

[291] The Pressler Amendment to the Foreign Service Act (Section 620e(e)) requires the administration to certify that any countries that receive U.S. assistance not possess nuclear devices. In 1990 the Bush administration could not certify that Pakistan met this requirement, and all aid was automatically suspended. However, U.S. AID has given more than U.S. $9 million since 1995 to NGOs operating in Pakistan and is planning to continue this indirect assistance.

renewal of economic aid to Pakistan.[292] Among the new programs announced by Albright were $10 million from the Agency for International Development (AID) for family planning, education, literacy, and nutrition; $10 million in food aid under the Food for Peace program; and a new Overseas Private Investment Corporation agreement to facilitate U.S. investment in Pakistan. None squarely addressed issues of violence against women or reform of the criminal justice system.

However, when Pakistan tested several nuclear devices in May 1998, all non-emergency assistance to Pakistan was again automatically stopped except for a congressional exception allowing Pakistan to buy American wheat.

Other Bilateral Assistance

The largest bilateral donor to Pakistan is Japan, which annually provides more than $250 million and is also Pakistan's second-largest trade partner. Other major donor countries include the United Kingdom, France, Germany, Canada, and the Netherlands. Most of these countries have women in development policies or programs, many of which are translated into funding for girls' education, family planning programs, and maternal health initiatives. Little official development assistance goes toward reforming the criminal justice system or making the medicolegal procedure more accessible to all crime victims, including women.

The European Union

The European Community (E.C.) has become the world's fifth-largest aid donor, with more than 90 percent of its assistance in the form of grants. Pakistan has been one of the largest recipients of European Community aid in Asia. Currently, the European Community, through its European Investment Bank, is financing the construction of a hydropower complex and backing family planning programs in Pakistan. Although it has repeatedly stated its commitment to promoting women's status and its recognition of women in sustainable development, the E.C. does not have an explicit women in development program in Pakistan, and none of its current assistance is addressing violence against women or reform of the criminal justice system.

International Financial Institutions

In addition to direct bilateral assistance, Pakistan annually receives several million dollars from international and regional financial institutions such as the

---

[292] The Pressler Amendment does not preclude these new initiatives becuase this aid channeled through nongovernmental subcontractors.

World Bank, the International Monetary Fund, the Islamic Development Bank, and the Asian Development Bank.

In fiscal year 1997, the World Bank administered forty-two projects in Pakistan totaling more than $4.4 billion.[293] The bank's numerous goals in Pakistan include supporting fiscal adjustment, expanding access to improved social services, reforming the banking system, developing infrastructure, and improving governance. As a general matter, the World Bank has included in its operational policies and procedures a consideration of the "gender dimension of development." Specifically, the bank's gender policy is intended "to reduce gender disparities and enhance women's participation in the economic development of their countries by integrating gender considerations in its country assistance program."[294] Included in the strategies to implement this policy is a bank pledge to assist countries in "review[ing] and modify[ing] legal and regulatory frameworks to improve women's access to assets and services, and take institutional measures to ensure that legal changes are implemented in actual practice, with due regard to cultural sensitivity."[295] Built into the policy are review mechanisms to evaluate the bank's success in integrating gender into its operations.

Although it does not directly improve women's access to justice or the Pakistan government's response to violence against women, one bank program that does target women is its support of Pakistan's Social Action Program, a nationwide strategy to improve basic social services (elementary education, primary health care, population welfare, and rural water supply and sanitation) with an emphasis on poor, rural women. The bank's $250 million credit to the program focuses on building the government's capacity to deliver effective social service programs, increasing accountability, and improving governance.

The Asian Development Bank has also funded women in development projects in Pakistan, although none is currently being supported. In 1997, the Asian Development Bank loaned more than $500 million to Pakistan, with the bulk of assistance going to agriculture, infrastructure, and finance programs. Improving the status of women is one of the ADB's medium-term objectives, but beyond a one-time $200 million loan to the Pakistan government's Social Action Program, the bank's current operations in Pakistan are doing little to achieve this objective.

---

[293] World Bank, *Country Brief: Pakistan*, http://www.worldbank.org/html/extdr/offrep/sas/pakist.htm.

[294] World Bank, *Operational Policies & Procedures: The Gender Dimension of Development*, http://www.worldbank.org/aftdr/bp/GENDER/gndmndev.htm.

[295] Ibid.

The United Nations
　　The United Nations has maintained a resident coordinator in Pakistan since 1979. More than a dozen U.N. agencies currently operate in Pakistan, including the U.N. Children's Fund (UNICEF), the U.N. Development Programme (UNDP), the World Food Programme (WFP), the World Health Organization (WHO), and the International Labour Organisation (ILO). In total, the U.N. system gave $76.7 million to Pakistan in official development assistance through its various funds, programs, and agencies in 1997. Several of these agencies are working to improve women's status in Pakistan, and a few programs directly address violence against women. The U.N. has also created an inter-agency working group on gender and development in Pakistan, composed of representatives from donor governments and U.N. agencies working in Pakistan, to discuss progress of the Pakistan government's gender-related initiatives and review ways to strengthen the U.N.'s own gender work.

　　Among the U.N. agencies operating in Pakistan, the UNDP has the most comprehensive gender program. Describing its approach in terms of empowerment, UNDP Pakistan's gender program has been working with the government to change the status of Pakistani women by focusing on a number of concrete areas, including women's mobility, economic and social empowerment, access to credit, negative portrayals of women in the media, and enterprise development for rural women. Although UNDP/Pakistan recognizes the link between violence, women's low status, and barriers to sustainable development, none of its current operations directly addresses preventing violence, facilitating women's access to justice, or improving the state's response to violence against women.

　　The WHO also has many programs in Pakistan, but none of its current operations in Pakistan addresses violence against women and its health consequences. WHO has been working to incorporate gender into its work more generally. It recently initiated a multi-country research project into domestic violence against women with the purpose of increasing awareness of the issue among the health community and improving its capacity to identify, prevent, and respond to such violence; Pakistan, however, is not among the countries being studied. Other WHO programs include documenting and testing intervention strategies; developing a research manual for work in poor areas; setting up a database of research and data on the many forms of violence against women; and compiling an information package for health professionals on current information about violence against women. WHO has recognized the critical role the health community plays in responding to violence against women and plans to produce guidelines for health professionals who work with victims of violence. As of 1999 none of these initiatives was being conducted in Pakistan, however. WHO should, in light of the prevalence of unremedied violence against women in the country, include Pakistan in its programs on women and violence or design an initiative that responds specifically to the problems in this context in Pakistan.

VIII. CONCLUSION

Despite the alarmingly high incidence of rape and domestic violence in Pakistan, the government appears to be uninterested in limiting impunity for these acts. According to the Human Rights Commission of Pakistan at least eight women are raped every twenty-four hours nationwide. Estimates of the number of women who experience domestic violence range from 70 to 95 percent—the government's own Commission of Inquiry for Women reported that it "has been described as the most pervasive violation of human rights" in Pakistan. The statistical evidence notwithstanding, the state officials Human Rights Watch spoke to invariably denied the severity, indeed the existence, of the problem of violence against women. Moreover, on August 2, 1999, the upper house of parliament refused even to consider a resolution condemning the ritual practice of so-called honor killing that claims the lives of hundreds of women every year.

The dismissive official attitudes toward violence against women reflect institutionalized gender bias that pervades the state machinery, including the law enforcement apparatus. Partly as a result of deep-seated and widespread biases against women, the criminal justice system does not operate as an avenue for redress and justice for women victims of violence. Victims who turn to the system confront a discriminatory legal regime, venal and abusive police, untrained medicolegal doctors, incompetent prosecutors, and skeptical judges. The deplorable level of medicolegal services in the country is itself a sign of the government's lack of will to tackle the problem of violence against women. Medical evidence plays a unique and critical role in prosecutions of sex crimes, the majority of victims of which are women. Particularly in light of the requirements of Pakistani rape law, a well-functioning medicolegal system is a practical prerequisite for the successful prosection of rape and sexual assault.

A comprehensive program of concrete measures and a deliberate reversal of existing government attitudes and polices is required to afford women victims of violence an effective remedy and equal protection of law. At a minimum, the government must enact legislation that explicitly establishes domestic and other familial violence as crimes. The discriminatory Zina Ordinance should be repealed, and Pakistan's previous rape laws should be re-enacted with an amendment to make marital rape a criminal offense. Police, medicolegal doctors, and prosecutors should be trained in the proper procedures for handling rape, sexual assault and domestic violence cases in their respective professional capacities. The government should fund nongovernmental organizations to provide shelters, legal aid, counseling, and medical care for women victims of violence. The government of Pakistan is obligated, under its own constitution and international law, to take requisite steps to eliminate gender discrimination in the criminal justice system and to put an end to impunity for violence against women, itself a form of such discrimination.